I0461484

From Disbelief to Assurance, Vol.1

A Journey Toward Spiritual Mastery

Adria Gaebrialla

Bright Heart
Publishers

From Disbelief to Assurance, Vol. 1

A Journey Toward Spiritual Mastery

by Adria Gaebrialla

Copyright © 2022 by Adria Gaebrialla

Library of Congress Control Number: 2022915804

ISBN: 979-8-9868268-0-6 (Paperback)
ISBN: 979-8-9868268-2-0 (Hardcover)
ISBN: 979-8-9868268-1-3 (eBook)

Disclaimer: The events and conversations in this book actually happened and are described to the best of the author's ability. Many scenes are explicit and may be difficult for sensitive people. The author's intention is to expand awareness, not cause undue stress by exploring these controversial adult themes. Names and minor details have been changed to protect the privacy of individuals.

Cover artwork by: Kaitlee Creates: www.kaitleecreates.art

First Edition   Printed in the USA

Published by Bright Heart Publishers,
1911 Douglas Blvd, 85-363, Roseville, California, 95610, USA

For orders or permissions contact: Bright Heart Publishers,
brightheartpublishers@gmail.com, www.brightheartpublishers.com

Visit the Author's Website at http://www.AuthorAdriaGaebrialla.com

Assurance:

1) A positive declaration intended to give confidence;

2) *Freedom from doubt; belief in yourself, self-confidence in your abilities;*

3) The **certainty of the connection between a human being and Divine Source** *unlimited by belief or deed; a constant presence; a relationship* **which can never fail, be lost or broken.**

A Note to Readers...

I SHARE MY JOURNEY, straightforward and raw with embarrassing imperfections, hoping that it will inspire you to persevere on your path and reassure you, you're not alone.

I hope my story shows that whether you were born with your intuitive abilities turned on or not; you don't have to be a highly skilled psychic to get answers from the most reliable source—your Higher Self and Divine Wisdom.

There are many ways you can connect and receive wisdom from Spirit, a connection which can provide clarity relating to your specific personal challenges.

Know that "Seek and you shall find," and, "Ask and you shall receive," are two of the truest directives in the world.

Use these directives to help you open the doors your eyes can't see, discover your truth, and get guidance on your journey toward clarity, peace and freedom. ~ *Adria*

Contents

About the structure of this book —

How this book works...

THE CHAPTERS FLOW DIFFERENTLY than a typical book. I designed my structure, as described below, to make it easy for you to experience what I discovered from my perspective. You will see through my eyes, and hear my thoughts as these amazing, terrible, and remarkable situations occur—just as they unfolded for me.

~ IN THE FIRST SECTION of each chapter, I start with a short information section. I've written the introductions from my vantage point in the present, telling you about my past. Most often, I introduce the scene to provide clarity and context. Sometimes, I share my goals and intentions for the experiences that follow. Many times I went into a session with one expectation and something entirely different happened. My journey has been full of surprises!

~ IN THE SECOND SECTION of each chapter (after the "***"), I switch to present tense so you can immerse yourself in the adventure. It allows you to see what I saw, feel what I felt, and experience what I experienced, as if you were there.

~ IN THE THIRD SECTION of each chapter, ("Conclusions"), I share my reactions and what the experience meant to me. I make my best guess about the lesson opportunities presented, what insights I had, and what answers I received.

Sometimes additional questions came to mind after the experience. Sometimes there were no questions. Sometimes I was so overwhelmed by the enormity of what I had experienced that all I could do was attempt to make sense of it.

There are some things in this universe — there are no words for.

My spirit helpers and/or higher self, have answered most of the questions I have put to them. Please check in **Appendix A — Questions Answered** at the back of the book! There you will find a list of the chapter(s) where I found answers to some of my questions. Please note, there are a few questions whose answers I have not yet received. :)

~ AT THE END of each chapter, **Spiritual Skills** are listed, (i.e. Clairaudience, Clairtangency, Clairvoyance, Retrocognition, etc.). These indicate which intuitive abilities were illustrated in the chapter.

I believed for most of my life that I had no intuitive abilities, without realizing that I'd been developing my intuition all along. So I list these skills because knowing how they manifest is an important step to being able to recognize these abilities in yourself. You may receive more than you know!

The events that unfold in each chapter provide excellent examples of the many ways intuitive information can be received. Often these abilities come in subconsciously before we learn to use them consciously, with intention. The **Glossary** in the back of the book provides clear definitions for all the Spiritual Skills listed.

THE NUMBER OF DETAILS I share may surprise you, especially since my journey extends across so many years. Most of what I share is from my journals, which I've kept most of my life. Writing helps me think and process emotions and experiences. So writing about my experiences was partly how I dealt with them.

For most of the session work, I recorded what occurred during the appointments and often my reactions immediately afterward. The details the recordings provide, when added to my own notes, enhance the clarity and help with the sequence of events. Many of you may know, during session work, you are in an altered state of awareness, and the plethora of details that come in don't always make it back through all the layers to the conscious mind. This is why I made recordings.

WHAT YOU MAY FIND NOTICEABLY ABSENT from my book are the names of people, places, and things. In prior drafts, they were included, but I was asked to remove them because of complicated permissions and legalities. Because I like details and accuracy, I resisted this, but Spirit reminded me that the primary focus of my book is my story and my experiences. For clarity's sake and to protect people's privacy, fictitious names have also been used. But please keep in mind it doesn't matter where I was, or what people's names were. It is the Spiritual journey that matters most.

My years spent working on myself, studying, and decades of practice have made me an expert—*on myself*, and a few things I learned along the way.

I hope that sharing my experiences will help those of you who are also seeking answers. My intention is to encourage you to seek your own unique truth.

Reader Discretion Advised...

MANY PAST LIVES CONTAIN traumas, which may be one reason we tend not to remember them. But the energies from those traumas can affect us in the present and manifest as unexplained preferences, pains, and fears. Many of my experiences, which I describe in my books, contain explicit violence, have controversial and adult themes, and scenes that may be psychologically disturbing.

I have described each incident as accurately as possible for the sake of clarity and honesty. Since I am sensitive to violence, I've tried to keep the explicit details to a minimum. For me, remembering these situations was quite difficult.

Since these experiences were a part of my journey and helped shape the person I am today, I include them in order to present a complete picture. The lifetimes that contain violence (emotional, psychological or physical) I describe with just enough detail to illuminate what I learned from them.

Every event I share in this book, I include to serve a purpose, to illustrate my journey or to convey an essential truth. Some of these details may be difficult for sensitive people, so please be advised.

Acknowledgments

To all who have accompanied me on this everlasting journey of love,

— You KNOW who you are —

I express my most sincere

Gratitude and appreciation...

To all who journey into the light...

I was not born a psychic...

...Why am I here?

My stubborn, tenacious curiosity has always been a constant companion. As a sensitive, playful child, I loved exploring and taking things apart. I needed to know how things worked and why. Often, I spent time alone, reflecting, reading and figuring things out. I had many questions. The more I learned, the more curious I became. Curiosity was and is the driving force behind my journey and my books.

As I grew, I had many questions, and I wanted *answers*. My most significant questions were:

- Why are there so many traumas in my life?

- Why do I have scary nightmares, and my sister doesn't?

- Why do I seem to be different from everyone else? And worst of all...

- Why have I always been terrified of flushing the toilet?

My curiosity continued to grow as I did. But then I began noticing odd things happening. They were very subtle things, but they were definitely odd.

By junior high school, I still hadn't figured out what I wanted to be when I grew up. I felt lost, and my quest to find answers to my questions looked hopeless. I spent my lunchtimes in the library seeking explanations and escape from the discomfort of socializing with my peers.

In high school, my questions got deeper:

- Why am I here?

- What is my life's purpose?

I believed there was something important I needed to do, which made me feel even more like an oddity. I thought I was different because my life had been so difficult. There had been constant emotional upheaval, frequent moves to unknown cities, an unstable family life, and loss. All the challenges had left me fearful, but they had also forced me to learn a lot. The deep losses, including the death of loved ones, drove me to try to understand my existence.

I thought perhaps religion might provide some answers. My family's church had some explanations, but their responses were a little vague or didn't feel quite right to me. I had also explored other faiths and attended a variety of churches, but there were always pieces missing.

I wanted to know:

- What happens to me after I die?

- What is the purpose of my life?

- Do I have a soul? And How do I *know* I have a soul?

- If I have a soul, where does it go after my body dies?

- Why do some people see Angels and Auras while others can't?

- Why do only a few people have the verifiable ability to connect with Spirits/God?

- Can God talk directly to me or to anyone? (Instead of through another person)

- I was not born psychic (clairvoyant, clairsentient, etc.), but *can I learn to be?*

I wanted more than just to understand what other people *believed* to be true. I wanted the actual truth, full explanations in answer to my questions. I wanted proof, *verifiable* proof. I wasn't sure where my skeptical mindset had originated, but I figured if God or Spirit could really do miraculous things, then Spirit could give me all the proof I wanted.

Now I share with you my struggles, my process, how I started, and what I discovered in my quest for answers. I am surprised and grateful to admit that I have developed the ability to connect directly to my highest self, to channel wisdom from the Wise Ones, to sense and communicate with Spirits, animals, and more. I can sense energies around me and can do so intentionally, with control and without fear.

After years of practice, it feels natural for me to connect to Spirit, though many people may view the ability as extraordinary. My transformation was not sudden or shocking. It happened gradually as I studied, took classes, did counseling, and regression work, which helped me to come to terms with and release my issues. I continue to work on fresh challenges even now, for there are always deeper layers that emerge as I grow from each set of lessons. Like peeling an onion, I am removing layers to get to the deep core of my infinite self.

I hope you'll consider the possibility that there is more to you than you may have imagined. All is not as it seems. I invite you to take a step forward and shine a bright light on your experiences, past and present, so you may gain clarity and perspective. You can free yourself to attain the life you envision. You are a sacred being and are well worth the effort!

— *With Love, Adria*

"The journey of a thousand miles, begins with a single step..."

— Lao Tzu

The Start of the Journey...

March 1, 1979, 16 yrs. of age

SOMETIMES PEOPLE EXPERIENCE AN event that transforms how they look at life. They have a near-death experience, a serious injury, or perhaps a sudden loss or tragedy. For me, the incident which motivated me to start my journey was not traumatic, but miraculous. What happened was impossible to explain, and could never be mistaken as a coincidence. This miracle occurred when I was 16, and the validity of it inspired me to search earnestly for answers to the questions which had bothered me for a long time:

1) Why am I here? / Where did I come from?

2) What is my Life's Purpose?

3) What happens after I die? And,

4) Does God really exist?

***

TONIGHT, I AM IN MY ROOM uncharacteristically early because I'm sick and I just want to lie down or try to find a position where I can breathe easier. After propping up on pillows and putting the humidifier on, I am still gasping for air. I feel so alone. My mom is in her room watching TV, her door closed, grading her school papers as always. I have been sick so often that she doesn't get overly concerned anymore. When my lungs get congested, a trip to the doctor doesn't happen. Dealing with my asthma has gotten old for both of us. Maybe she thinks my illness is a ploy to get attention.

Consciously, I don't think I want to be sick, but perhaps subconsciously it's a wish for a more loving, nurturing relationship with her. My current respiratory congestion started last fall and has never completely healed. It's been six months and with the allergens of spring adding to the irritation of my clogged lungs, I'm sicker than when the cold started.

All my inhalers and medicines don't seem to help anymore. Even the humidifier turned on high, which fills my room with eucalyptus-scented fog and has my teen-idol posters melting into the damp walls, has made no difference. As I lay here, every breath a struggle, I feel the muscles between my ribs fatiguing, sore from forcing air into my congested lungs. Breathing at this moment feels like trying to sip a drink through a ten-foot straw.

After struggling for months, I'm exhausted and want to give up. I feel so helpless, so hopeless. I let myself stop breathing, craving rest, no longer up to the challenge of life. I can only pause for a few seconds, but it seems to help my tired rib muscles. Scenes from my life pop in and out of my mind, memories of prior breathing struggles. I feel like I'm at the end of my rope. I have a choice at this moment; I am at a crossroads. Do I fight to stay alive, or is it time for me to go?

I wonder whether life or death is my decision, or is that the province of a higher power? I'm not a religious person, though I've explored the spiritual concepts of many faiths. All faiths have something to offer, but none seem to have definitive answers to my questions. With nothing to lose, I decide to ask for help. Rolling my eyes upward, I say,

"God, if you are really up there, either take me now or heal me."

It is a simple, clear, and direct request, which leaves the final decision in the hands of whatever higher power might be listening. I fall asleep in my room sometime afterward, waiting for an answer.

Unsure of how long I've been sleeping, I wake up suddenly in the dark of night. Not wanting to stir, I keep my eyes closed and stay still so I won't start coughing again. I'm alert and awake, though I don't know what disturbed me. What's unusual is that I seem highly tuned-in to my surroundings. Somehow I can clearly see the outlines of my furniture, the shape of my body under the blankets, the bookcases on the wall above my head, yet my eyes are closed. It's as if there's a movie playing on the inside of my eyelids. This is something new and different.

As I watch, a beautiful, bright blue light pours down from the ceiling above me. It is like shiny liquid, flowing toward me, landing in the center of my stomach. I sense tingling warmth as the light quickly spreads like a wave throughout my body. When the wave reaches my lungs, I feel instant relief—I can breathe!

I take great gulping breaths of air, totally wheeze-free. The liquid energy completely fills my being with warmth and glows, like a cocoon of vibrant light radiating out four to five inches surrounding my entire body. The glowing blue continues on for what seems to be quite a while. I can't really tell for how long. It's one of those experiences where time slows down and has little meaning.

This incident feels like it's more than just physical. Some higher force, Spirit, or something, must have heard me. My request to either die or be completely healed has been fulfilled. I received an answer! I wasn't expecting that.

The blue light slowly fades, and I sleep again. I wake up the next morning and I am completely well. I have a couple of stray coughs, but no cold, no more wheezing, and I can breathe!

***

CONCLUSIONS:

After that event, I stopped taking all my asthma medications with no harmful consequences. My wellness lasted for years, which was amazing for someone who tended to have two or more colds every season. The asthma was gone!

It had been impossible for my doubting, skeptical, scientific mind to explain the incident away as coincidence. There'd been too much evidence which pointed to the fact that I had not imagined my experience and even if I had, the results were undeniable. I'd been able to breathe immediately and was well the next day. No doubt. No denying it. No more medications. Nothing like this had ever happened to me before, nor had I heard of anything like this happening to anyone I knew.

Someone or something had heard me. Something greater than myself had healed me—just as I had asked.

The experience was especially remarkable considering I'd struggled with asthma allergies, and sensitivities my entire life. I told no one about what happened, not even my mother. I was afraid people would think I was crazy, or that I had made it up. They might have attributed my experience to a religious upbringing, or thought I was dabbling in metaphysics, or some other mystic art. But that had not been the case.

After the blue light healing, I paid more attention. That experience had been a loud and clear answer, which I could not dismiss as a coincidence. I tried to find an explanation for what happened to me in metaphysical books, but found no answers. None of them mentioned a healing light.

I also tried to find something that could duplicate the vivid blue color I'd seen. I shined lights through blue glass, collected paint samples, and urgently searched for physical objects that could replicate that vibrant electric blue energy, but found nothing that came close. I HAD to find out more. I needed to know what that Blue Light was!

Could I ask for it again? Who had heard me? How did I get in touch with them? So many questions flooded my mind, adding to the ones already there. I needed to find out the truth about the way things really worked. I was no longer content to just wait for answers. I started actively searching immediately.

After receiving such irrefutable evidence, my motivation was off the scale. It's one thing to read about miracles, but it's quite another to experience one!

Section One – Fear and Uncertainty

I am starting to notice intermittent odd events and

weird coincidences happening.

This collection of apparently random,

unrelated incidents are starting to make me wonder,

Giving rise to questions, yet unanswered.

1

Recurring Nightmares

May 5, 1968, 5 yrs. (of age)

Author's Note:

In 2013, my career as I knew it was over. A series of injuries, one after another, made it impossible for me to continue working. Suddenly, I was retired, in pain, and at a crossroads, wondering what to do next. As many do, I returned to what had helped me before. I sought comfort and guidance from spirit, after having avoided all things spiritual for many years. Who else could answer my unanswerable questions? It occurred to me if I reviewed where I had been, I might discover which way to turn. This book is the result.

While assembling the pieces, I wondered when the intuitive (psychic) events in my life had initially begun. I recalled several odd things that had happened to me during my childhood and early teen years. I'd experienced nightmares, déjà vu feelings, and a few other strange situations. But honestly, I hadn't been paying attention until after the blue light had healed me.

These early events had been explained and dismissed by my family, who told me that these were normal situations which everyone endured. Their reasons never quite made sense to me, but I ignored the incidents as they suggested. However, once I put them into context with the other oddities I'd encountered on my spiritual journey, the events I had discounted grew in importance. It was like finding lost pieces to an old jigsaw puzzle.

So before I continue with what happened after the "Start of the Journey," what follows are a few things that came up before being healed by the blue light... ~ Adria

----

THE ODD MYSTERIES OF MY LIFE began at age five or six.

I had some scary recurring nightmares. Because they kept coming back repeatedly, I always wished I knew why they did, and what they meant. But mostly, I just wanted them to stop! I would wake up screaming, absolutely terrified, out of breath and sweating like I'd been running for my life. My mother, the light sleeper, hadn't enjoyed my screaming wake-up calls either.

These two nightmares kept recurring, primarily during my during my childhood and late teen years. Once in a while, they even crept into the nights of my adulthood...

***

NIGHTMARE #1: I'm in the bathroom. I flush the toilet, but it doesn't stop running. It's overflowing, and water keeps pouring over the edge of the bowl. I call for help because I can't get the bathroom door open. The bathroom is filling up with water and sewage. Soon I'm swimming in it and the water level is inches from the ceiling. I'm about to drown when I wake up screaming; my heart is pounding and I'm out of breath. This dream is always the same and is always terrifying.

NIGHTMARE #2: I am in my room looking at a tiny clear plastic box that is square and lined with cotton. I get these boxes from the dentist every time he extracts a tooth. He puts my pulled teeth in a box so I can take them home and give them to the tooth fairy.

As I open the little box, a tiny grain of sand rolls off the cotton onto the table, but it doesn't stay there. The sand rolls toward me. As it rolls, other particles attach to it and it grows like a snowball rolling down a slope, except my snowball is reddish-brown mud. Startled, I back away, but it seems to follow me. Now I'm outside and it keeps growing larger and is picking up straw, debris, more mud and momentum as it continues chasing me.

Soon I'm running fast as I can, yet it's still gaining! The mud ball is over 10-12 feet tall and looking like a giant rust-colored ball of adobe, with straw and junk sticking out of it. I keep trying to dodge it, change my pathway and go faster, but nothing seems to help. It's about to roll over and kill me when I wake up, out of breath, usually screaming—definitely scared to death.

CONCLUSIONS:

Dreams are often inexplicable and whimsical, but the dreams I had were far from delightful. Mine were terrifyingly real.

The first dream occurred many times when I was little, so naturally I became fearful of flushing the toilet. As a child, I could usually get my big sister to do it. Whenever I used a public restroom, I always made sure that the stall door was unlatched, so I could run out the door the moment after I flushed the toilet. I did not have a fear of water, elimination problems, nor was I scared of being locked in the bathroom, just flushing. I'm sure my sister thought I was crazy but, since I was her little sister she probably thought that, anyway.

The second dream happened when I was older, but it felt even more menacing. It also tended to start over again as soon as I fell back to sleep, which was extremely disturbing. The endless replay of my worst nightmare made it really hard for me to want to go back to sleep! One night after the mud-ball almost killed me several times, I tried to find a way to clear my mind of the frightening images and came up with this soothing visualization:

> Breathing deeply, I picture a beautiful field full of golden poppies, an expansive meadow surrounded by gently rolling foothills, with an enormous solitary oak tree standing in the center. I imagine myself walking toward the tree. As I get closer, I notice that the wooden slats attached to the trunk create a ladder. Excited, I realize it leads to a tree house and I start climbing up, but before I get to the top to see what marvels await, I fall back to sleep.

As an adult, I discovered that, spiritually speaking, nightmares are important because they connect to deeper issues. Nightmares are the subconscious screaming a message to us that we have not understood any other way. Often the messages are first delivered in other, gentler ways. But when we don't listen, the subconscious turns up the volume. I guess I hadn't been listening, and my nightmares were trying to get through to me. They were definitely not random since they happened over and over again, the same way every time.

The mud ball dream had provided at least one benefit. It had helped me to find a way to keep the frightening images from replaying in my mind. Being able to change my vision and calm myself during moments of stress ended up helping me in many situations later in life.

Questions:

- Why did I have these nightmares, ones in which my life was threatened?

- Why did they keep coming back over and over again?

Spiritual Skills Present: Clairvoyance, Meditation

The Museum

September 1, 1971, 9 yrs.

THESE SMALL BUT SIGNIFICANT EVENTS occurred when my mom, my sister and I went to a museum which had an extensive collection of Egyptian artifacts. My mom had always been fascinated by ancient Egypt. What was unique about this museum was that they had designed a few of the buildings to realistically replicate the architectural designs of ancient Egypt...

***

I WALK WITH MY FAMILY toward an entrance, turn the corner and see a building where two enormous pylons stand tall. They resemble the grand columns often found in the magnificent Temples of Egypt[1]. The closer I get, the more freaked out I feel because these structures seem very familiar but also frightening to me. I experience a major case of déjà vu at the sight of these pylons.

I am so scared that I almost cannot go into the building. I think it is weird that I have never been here before, never seen these before, never been to Egypt, and yet I'm panic-struck. Why? Why does the sight of the Temple entrance haunt me so much?

Once inside, I walk around the museum out of focus in an uneasy daze. I am so relieved when I exit with Mom through a side door which leads to a beautiful garden. In the center of the lush grounds is a bookstore where they have information about Egypt and a gift section that has souvenirs, statues and replicas of tomb paintings done on papyrus. My mom buys me a cartoon book about the life of Buddha, which I become fascinated with. I find it so intriguing that I can't put it down. I have never heard about the teachings of Buddha before, plus I am not a comic book reader, so it seems very strange to me that I am so enchanted by this book.

As much as I feel upset and repelled by the pylons, I am equally calmed and drawn to the bookstore, the Buddha Comic book, and the gardens.

***

CONCLUSIONS:

These incidents left me disoriented and questioning why. Why had I been so scared at the site of the building? Why had these images haunted me so much? I'd never experienced such a powerful reaction to a place which I had not visited before. Had it been just a coincidence, or was something important connected to these places? I had also felt strangely drawn to the gardens. I wished I could stay or go back there again, and longed to find a copy of that comic book, since it got lost during one of our many moves.

Questions:

- Were these random, inexplicable events coincidences, or were they something more meaningful?

- These incidents were not fearful dreams. Why were these strange things happening?

- How could I find answers to explain these strong uprushes of feelings?

Spiritual Skills Present: Claircognizance, Clairsentience

[1] —Many years later, still searching for an explanation, I discovered that the structures at Philae, Edfu and Karnak to be very similar to what I had seen at the museum

3

Déjà View

June 30, 1972, 10 yrs.

MY SISTER AND I WERE usually sent to stay with my great aunt and uncle every summer. My mom was an elementary school teacher and consequently wanted her summers to be kid-free so she could have some time to herself. To be honest, we were also happy to have some time away from her. My Aunt Dottie and Uncle Joe had never had children, so it worked out well for everyone.

During the summer after fifth grade, my aunt and uncle took us on a summer-long, cross-country driving trip. We even got out of school early in May, which was exciting. I loved summer, so an even longer one was wonderful! On this trip, I saw more than museums, historical sites and gorgeous scenery...

***

AFTER DRIVING THROUGH THE FLATLANDS and seeing miles and miles of wheat fields, we stop at a roadside quick-market for supplies and a lunch break. The market is shaped like a half-cylinder, a sheet metal building resembling an old army barracks. It is nothing remarkable and there is no interesting reason to stop here; it is just a random place to pick up groceries, have lunch in the RV and then be on the road again. We are on our way to visit my uncle's sister.

What's odd is what happens to me when I go inside the market with my aunt to shop for groceries. Suddenly, I seem to know where everything is. As my aunt reads off the items on her shopping list, I lead her to where each item is located in the market. I *know* where *every* item is; which aisle it is on and even which shelf. As I am doing this, it's like I'm on autopilot.

CONCLUSIONS:

I hadn't realized until after we stepped outside that something very odd had come over me in that store. Prior to the trip, I had not traveled outside my home state and I definitely had not visited the state we had stopped in. There was no way I could have known *anything* about that store, let alone where every item was stocked. This hadn't been a mere case of déjà vu, where something seemed vaguely familiar, like a place or a face. While I had been inside that store in that odd mind-space, I tapped into some kind of knowledge that was impossible for me to be aware of.

As a young gal, I didn't know what to think of my strange experience, but the memory of it has stayed very vivid. I have been puzzled over this incident for a long time. Maybe the mystery of the experience was the purpose of it, to motivate me to discover answers...

Spiritual Skills Present: Claircognizance, Clairsentience, Intuition

4

Invitation of the heart

October 3, 1975, 13 yrs.

AFTER MY PARENTS GOT DIVORCED, my mom did not return to her church or any other. I think she blamed some of her marital problems on her former religion and their practices. Though she no longer wished to attend any worship services, she told me and my sister that we were free to explore any belief systems we were drawn to.

This granted my sister and me religious freedom that not all children were allowed to experience. I took advantage of that opportunity and investigated a variety of faiths. Armed with the questions I wanted answered, I went to church. However, I usually ended up leaving with more questions than I came in with.

This incident occurred when I visited a local Sunday school...

***

I AM TRYING OUT the local churches within walking distance from home. At Sunday school this morning, the teacher asks those of us who haven't accepted Jesus into their heart if we want to do so right now. I decide to give it a try. I'm not sure I understand, but being new and shy, I don't want to embarrass myself by saying no or let on that I don't get it. I feel at a distinct disadvantage being both a spiritual beginner and in an unfamiliar church. But I really want to learn and know what this is all about.

We close our eyes and pray. We repeat the words the teacher tells us. Then we ask Jesus into our hearts and wait... and wait... I am not sure what to expect, but after a little while, I can feel a slight heat radiating from the center of my chest. It is definitely warm and tangible. It feels good, but it is brief, so brief that afterwards I am not even sure it really happened.

***

CONCLUSIONS:

Now in looking back at this, this may have been a first gentle knock on the door. It was nothing too earthshaking, enough to feel *something*, but not so much that I would be frightened by what happened.

Questions:

- Had Jesus actually come into my heart?

- I had felt warmth in the area of my heart, but was that warmth Jesus?

- Will I be able to talk to and hear Him now?

Spiritual Skills Present: Clairempathy, Clairtangency

5

Wellness Expo

May 31, 1976, 13 yrs.

MY MOTHER OCCASIONALLY took us to a Wellness Faire where vendors sold the latest in health products, and intuitive practitioners offered a variety of psychic readings. For my sister and I, it was an outing, something we rarely got to enjoy. The food at these expos tended to be weird, like burgers made from soybeans. They were the latest in health food, but they tasted kind of gross to me.

Still, the Expo had been more fun and interesting than *another* museum...

***

AS WE ENTER THE EXPO, I notice it is filled with lots of curtained spaces with tables and sales people dressed both simply and theatrically. Visitors flit from booth to booth, exploring all the options. The smell of exotic aromas and incense wafts through the air, and reminds me of the natural food restaurants that are getting popular now.

Mom gives my sister and me enough money for us both to get two readings at the booths, which is not normal for her. Maybe she wants some extra time to herself. She tells us where and when to meet her later, then off we all go in different directions. I check out every booth to see what is being offered so I can make the most of this special treat.

After much consideration, I choose something called psychometry for my first reading. The guy doing it says he'll read my watch by holding it and then talk to me about myself and my future. Since I will start high school soon, any hint of a future direction is welcome. He takes my watch and after a few minutes, tells me I am going to be a nurse, doctor or some kind of healer. He sees me practicing in an institutional setting. I assume he means some type of medical professional. I hope. Maybe.

It's all over quickly and I feel like I didn't get my money's worth after this reading. How will I know if he's right? I may forget what he said before it comes true. But what if I don't forget and I keep thinking about what he said and then lose time waiting for his predictions to come true? Will I make wrong choices because I'm trying to make my future happen the way he says it will? Maybe this reading thing wasn't a good idea. I'm not sure I want to know someone else's ideas about what my future holds. When choosing my next reading, I must be more cautious. I'd like to get information that will help me get clearer rather than more confused.

I look around carefully to make my final selection of the day. I really want something that I can hold in my hand and take away with me. If I get a reading that I can validate, something real and more tangible than words spoken and soon forgotten, I think it will be much better. After observing closely, I decide to go to a lady who is doing aura readings. I choose her mainly because every person she helps is walking away with written information and a drawing, probably the results of her reading.

She and her customers seem to have lively, friendly discussions too.

I go up and ask her for a reading. She asks me to sit down and I pay the fee. She pulls out a piece of paper which has an outline of a person sitting cross-legged, pre-printed on the top of the page. Then she starts writing. She never says another word to me. She barely even looks at me. I am beginning to feel like I made another poor decision. She keeps writing and fills up both sides of the paper. Then she pulls out some colored pencils and draws lines around the diagram at the top. She finishes and hands me the piece of paper. Done.

Bewildered, I say thank you and walk away. I am mad at myself for wasting my treat by making lousy choices. Mom wants to leave as soon as my reading is done, so I don't have time to look at what the aura reader wrote until I'm in the car on the way home.

As I read what she wrote, I am astonished at how accurate her description of my personality is. She also describes the colors of the lights she saw around my body, with an explanation of their significance. I am amazed. She had barely looked at me; it seemed like she was ignoring me the whole time, but somehow she picked up this information about me and it's correct. Had she actually seen all these different colors around me?

CONCLUSIONS:

This was an interesting and thought-provoking day, one I did not forget.

As far as the readings I received, my future, as described by the guy who did psychometry with my watch, didn't come true as he predicted. His words had impacted me since I never forgot them. His vision of my future hovered in the back of my mind, and may have affected my thoughts and influenced some of my key decisions. Of course, since I was 13 years old when I got the reading done, there was no way for me to know at the time if his predictions were accurate.

In the years since his reading, I spent a lot of time searching for direction, changing course several times, always wondering and worrying if I was choosing the right path. During my times of confusion and stress, his predictions would pop back into my mind, which created more uncertainty. There was no way to determine how much his predictions had influenced my life-changing decisions. Now, in retrospect, I believe that having someone else tell you about your future can be a risky thing to do.

To be fair and honest, part of what he hinted at had come about. I did eventually become a Reiki Master, which is a type of energy worker. But I never became a nurse, doctor or healer practicing in an institutional setting.

The aura reader had been amazing. How had she known that stuff about me? How had she received her information? She had barely seemed to notice me, at least with her physical senses. How had she done it? That reading so startled me, I felt there had to be more to this psychic stuff than I'd originally thought. It seemed that there were many different ways people could receive intuitive information.

If these kinds of readings were examples of applied metaphysics, then maybe I should give them more attention than I had before. It seemed like learning more about spiritual practices would help me find answers to my endless list of questions.

I had already looked at some metaphysical books and thought they sounded similar to the religious teachings that I'd read. But the books I'd found had not described the different kinds of readings people had been doing at the Faire.

While exploring various faiths, I had discovered that there were always questions to which they had no reply. I'd received some responses, but they were based on religious teachings or opinion, not fact, or first-hand experience. I was never told, "There are some things we don't know or that we're not sure of yet, but we invite you to look for your answers with us." It would have been awesome if anyone had ever said that to me.

Questions:

- Now that I want to learn more about metaphysics — where do I begin?

- What are some good, uplifting and accurate books on the subject, books that I can understand?

Spiritual Skills Present: Clairvoyance, Claircognizance, Precognition, Psychometry, Aura reading

6

It's all in a face...?

July 1, 1977, 14 yrs.

During family visits down south, Mom often took us to an amazing museum of antiquities near the coast. This special place had been designed and built as a full-sized replica of an ancient Roman villa, complete with gardens, fountains and pools. Whenever we visited there, it felt different from other museums. It was like stepping back into ancient times.

On rare occasions, when just a few people were present, we could feel the ambiance of the past envelop us the moment we stepped into the main garden. We would stroll down meandering pathways surrounded by lush plant growth, breathing in the rich smell of fresh earth. Orderly hedges and colorful flowers wound harmoniously alongside ancient sculptures, mosaics, and fountains, which added to the sense of timelessness.

Each step deeper into the landscape took us further back into the past. The splashing water of the reflecting pool fountains in the center of the garden created waves of peaceful sounds which soothed nearby guests. Bright white columns stood in perfect rows next to elegant hallways. They had painted the outer garden walls with nature scenes so realistic that they looked more like windows than cement. Everything had been precisely set in mathematical perfection to create splendid views from any location in the garden.

This place felt like a sacred site to me. Our visits usually filled me with peace, but on this occasion...

WE ARRIVE EARLY and after a relaxing walk in the garden, Mom and I make our way up the marble steps to the main building where all the exhibit rooms open onto the Inner Courtyard. Here, more statues, gardens, and lovely fountains delight the senses, inviting us to slow our pace.

In the first few chambers, I am impressed by the ancient jewelry and small statues on display. The intricate details of each piece, and the superior quality of the materials, are a testament to the skill of the artisans who created them so long ago. I follow my mom into the next room, which has a collection of life-sized ancient Greek statues. The cool marble figures, thousands of years old, look blankly back at me as I gaze at each face, wondering about their life and experiences. I see that some statues are representations of gods and goddesses whose expressions and clothing are in keeping with their ascribed personality.

Then I come to a section where fragments of statues are on display. There are a few busts that show the heads and shoulders of several subjects. Next featured is a row of heads, the only salvageable remains of once magnificent works of art.

I feel peculiarly drawn to some of the faces immortalized in marble. One of them is a very detailed carving of a male who has a bit of a surly expression; he looks very familiar. Next, in the lineup, is a woman's face, not as well preserved, then another sculpture of a smiling youth. Neither of these two strike me like the surly man.

Next, my eyes come to rest on a youthful man's face, even more familiar to me than the first one. Why do I feel like this, like I know these people? Is it an artistic technique? My mom has moved on while I remain rooted to the spot in front of that face, still staring at it like I've seen a ghost. As with the rest of the faces, I wonder about him.

But then things change. Voices drift into my head, as if they are sounds from moments in the life of this man. I hear a female screaming in distress and several male voices shouting. I hear them but can't understand what they're saying. I feel something terrible has happened. In my mind's eye, I am viewing a scene in the middle of a battle. There's an enormous wall with a wooden ladder leaning against it. I sense lots of noise and confusion. I seem to be climbing the ladder when I feel a sharp physical pain, like a spear, in the center of my chest. It seems like there is someone behind me...

Then, as quickly as they began, the sounds and visions fade. The uprush of feelings remain: grief, anger, sadness, confusion, and longing. Coming out of this, I am stunned and trying to make sense of what just happened. I search for the name of this person. I find the name plate; it says this sculpture is of Alexander the Great. What?!

A large group of visitors enters the room and people are crowding in to see, so I finally move on, still in a daze. What did I just hear? What is going on? I need time to think. I walk mechanically through the rest of the wing. Nothing has the same effect on me. I break away from my mom later that day and go back to the same spot to look, watch and wait to see if what I experienced will happen again, but it doesn't. Before we leave, I stop in the museum gift shop. I search for anything and everything I can find about Alexander, trying to find a clue as to what I had seen and felt.

***

Conclusions:

After this experience, I searched for years for information about Alexander, thinking that what I had seen was in some way connected to one of the events in his life.

In the years that followed, every time I visited the museum, I would stop in to see his statue. No other statue had elicited such a response.

Although, once in the same museum, there had been a larger-than-life bust of the goddess Athena, who also seemed vaguely familiar. She had been created wearing a helmet and armor and had such a lifelike face! It almost seemed like the statue looked a little like me. I suppose there aren't that many unique faces in the world, but it was weird to look at a statue and see a face similar to my own.

The battle scene vision I saw remained clear in my mind and kept me looking for answers, trying to discover what it was all about. Every time I visited a bookstore, I looked through the ancient history section, hoping to find an answer. Hopefully, someday, I would fully understand. The vision was so vivid, with colors, sights and sounds, like a movie playing in my head, one that I would not easily forget. It felt so real, like I had been there.

Questions:

- What did I see, an actual scene from a life, or did I make it all up?

- Why was it so vivid, and why did so many emotions rush in?

- Was it more than just imagination or visualization?

Spiritual Skills Present: Clairaudience, Claircognizance, Clairempathy, Clairsentience, Clairvoyance, Intuition, Psychometry, Retrocognition

7

Singing in Sync

May 5, 1978, 15 yrs.

WHEN I WAS IN HIGH SCHOOL, my bedtime was still 7:30 p.m., which, of course, I despised. To get around this rule, I would go to my room and turn the lights out, but then I stayed up as long as I wanted. I did this because I was a teenager and a night owl. My mom required my early bedtime. It was for her sake, not mine. She needed quiet after her challenging days teaching elementary school kids, something for which she was not well-suited.

Consequently, I spent a lot of time hanging out in my room. Sometimes I read by the light of a candle or a flashlight. Eventually, I got a small transistor radio so I could quietly listen to radio shows or music. My other option was to listen to albums on my record player, which I did, especially my favorite summertime music.

One night, I must have drifted off with my radio on...

***

I'M DREAMING I AM IN A NIGHTCLUB where my favorite singer is singing one of my favorite songs. We know each other, and I am there singing along with him. I can clearly see the nightclub, the people sitting at small tables, and the lights shining through a smoky haze. I smell the smoke and cologne and hear the music.

The song has some poignant lyrics in it which bring tears to my eyes, similar to what happens to me when I'm awake.

While I am experiencing this vivid dream, I become aware of someone else starting to sing, then realize it is my own present day voice singing out loud. I wake up to discover that I am singing along in perfect time with the radio, which is playing the exact same song, at the same moment as the one in my dream. I struggle to stay tuned into my dream where I feel so close to the singer, but I can't. The dream fades and I wake up to find tears running down my face. It was so real; it felt like I was really there...

***

Conclusions:

The vibrant quality of that dream probably hadn't been unusual, but finding myself in perfect sync with the radio in the physical realm had been. Sleep singing with the radio had been a cool new adventure. It made me wonder, had the dream happened first, then my mind worked the song into it, or had the song prompted the dream? Either way, it seemed like I had been in the dream for a lot longer than the length of a song. It had been so lifelike, as if I was really there: seeing, hearing, and smelling, moving in a body, with all my senses functioning. I had talked with people at the club, sensed connections and relationships, and I had been singing along with the singer. It felt like I had been in that club for hours rather than a few moments. I had experienced an altered perception of time.

That strange and wonderful feeling of being in perfect sync with others had happened to me before with music, but in a different way. While playing in band, I felt the same eerie sensation of random variables falling into place. Whenever we rehearsed in band, I would hear an ideal version of the music playing inside my head: every part played in perfect time and pitch, every harmony just right.

On rare occasions, when all the people in band played just right, then the band's version of the piece would match up with the perfect ideal playing in my mind. The resulting sense of harmony was incredible and hard to describe. Time slowed down, and I had a heightened awareness of everything, even of how my fingers were moving on the keypads. I could hear notes coming from the other instruments, while the sound from my horn felt like it was an extension of my heart singing, an audible sound from my soul. Experiencing such synchronicity made the idea that we are all connected much more believable to me and made my dream seem like it could be an alternate reality.

My dream experience had been remarkable, one in which some subconscious part of me had been alert, aware, and in sync with the outer world. For such a brief experience, it had remained incredibly clear, and I missed the reality of it. I felt like I belonged, like it connected me to a place that felt like home.

Questions:

- What purpose did this experience serve?

Spiritual Skills Present: Astral Projection/Out of Body, Clairalience, Clairaudience, Claircognizance, Clairempathy, Clairsentience, Clairvoyance, Synchronicity

8

Just a book...

August 8, 1978, 16 yrs.

THIS SIMPLE CHOICE was something that changed my life. It was not a strange, inexplicable occurrence, like some of the other incidents I have described. It was a casual activity, on an ordinary day, doing a simple thing like shopping. I bought a book. I just *randomly* found it while I was on a family vacation. However, this coincidental purchase, and the ideas I found in this book, ended up being transformational, and enabled me to change my life in more ways than I imagined possible...

***

MY MOTHER AND I are in town for a family visit and decide to explore an international street fair. There are food and craft booths from every country. We stop to browse at a book vendor. I am not really looking for anything in particular; I'm just waiting for my mom, who is an avid book reader. I like to read, but I am a teenager on summer vacation and I'm more interested in going to the beach.

I look through the rack of science fiction books just in case there is something about my favorite sci-fi TV shows or movies. I find a book which has people on the cover who are wearing tunics, which reminds me of a sci-fi movie I liked. The summary captures my interest when I discover the characters do some time traveling. I enjoy TV shows and movies which bring historical events to life. often by having the characters travel through time. I buy the book, begin reading it, and find I can't put it down.

My new book describes a highly developed, spiritually advanced society of the future. Its citizens have learned to approach life from an enlightened perspective. They have an easy camaraderie and respect for each other and are happy to work cooperatively together to create a peaceful world community. They have eliminated the situations which used to divide people from each other. Things like war, greed, poverty, and prejudice don't exist anymore. People are no longer fearful and lonely, but peacefully interdependent. Nature has bounced back with enthusiasm in response to coordinated efforts to clean-up what prior human populations had done to damage the environment. Earth's splendor has been restored. Caring communities which uplift and support their citizens' development are now the new norm. The quality of life on earth, for all its inhabitants, has improved dramatically.

This idea of a culture, which empowers and inspires each person to expand their awareness and develop spiritually as they choose, is very appealing to me. A joyful populace with deep connections to each other, that lovingly supports the personal progress of every citizen without judgement or censure sounds wonderful. Their society also provides a network of wise mentors and supportive friends to ensure that they meet everyone's needs, and forget no one. People have all the support they need to help them evolve as quickly as possible. Their society has created the ultimate freedom for their people.

Released from the concerns and fears of providing for their daily needs, these future citizens spend their time doing healthful things they enjoy. They support and encourage each other and the community, and still have time to work on their own personal development. This amazing idea feels totally right to me. (It would have been so nice to have that much support during my current life challenges!)

The people in this book find that their intuitive (psychic) abilities grow stronger as they expand their spiritual awareness. Each individual strives to grow, being limited only by how much they want to improve themselves, and how strongly they believe in their ability to do so.

They model their society on the idea that everything is part of a connected whole. Since they are part of each other, the community supports everyone's efforts, which uplifts them all. Mistakes and challenges are happily welcomed as opportunities for growth. Once people learn to identify and change their harmful habitual thought and behavior patterns, their awareness expands. As society members evolve, their ability to demonstrate the principles of unconditional love and oneness also grows.

Because of the philosophy described in this book, I finally find a few answers to some of the questions I've been asking. To imagine living in such a supportive and nurturing environment is life-changing for me. I talk about these ideas to my friends, family, and anyone who will listen; perhaps too much. I'm so excited about the possibility of such an ideal life and world that I can't help it.

***

CONCLUSIONS:

Ultimately, the concepts presented in the book helped me to understand that I needed to learn to respect, accept, and love myself as an important part of the universe. I also needed to come to terms with the fact that the ideal society portrayed in the book did not yet exist. While I was immersed in reading the book, it became so real to me it was hard to adjust my frame of mind back to the real world of today. Someday soon, I hoped greater numbers of people would choose to create a more peaceful, uplifting way of interacting with each other, and in the meantime, I would try to do my part.

This idealistic model had been so thoroughly motivating that I decided to spend my life becoming the best me I could. I devoted more time to my own personal evolution. I began by learning to resolve my personal issues and changing my negative habits. Once I started applying some of the metaphysical principles I had learned to my daily life, I was better able to take my challenges in stride, knowing that everything was unfolding as it should.

Questions:

- The concepts in the book had also helped to answer a couple of my original questions: "If I am not born with psychic gifts, can I develop them?" and "Can anybody develop these skills?" The book suggested it was a possibility. If I could figure out how to take some of the action steps that they used in the book, maybe I could improve my life. I might even find some proof along the way. It just felt right to me.

- Although my goal had never been to become psychic, it might be fun to have some intuitive abilities. But I was a little afraid of developing these types of skills. Would I be bombarded with more information than I could handle without being able to stop it? I already felt overwhelmed and uncomfortable when inundated by too much noise, too much visual input, and crowds of too many people. I would not want my senses to be flooded with more information without being able to control it.

- What I thought I could manage, was to learn to live in peace with myself and be my true self during my daily activities. To live and work with like-minded, spiritually aware people, without having to pretend to be something I was not, would be fantastic. It just wanted to heal my past hurts, and to fix what was broken within me. Could I find ways to heal my past so I could feel better in my present?

Spiritual Skills Present: Claircognizance, Divine timing, Intuition, Synchronicity

9

Blue Light Healing

March 1, 1979, 16 yrs.

Author's Note:

In keeping with the chronological order of events, it's important to note that the blue light healing, which started my spiritual investigations occurred at this point, at 16 years of age. (See "The Start of the Journey").

Putting this healing incident into its correct place in the sequence of spiritual experiences should provide some context.

I had experienced so little, and understood even less when this happened. For me, the context makes this miracle even more astonishing... ~ Adria

10

The Golden Light

November 20, 1979, 17 yrs.

JUST BEFORE MY SENIOR YEAR in high school, big changes had come to pass. My mom had broken her ten-year communication blackout and called my dad, pleading for his help in talking my sister out of getting married at the age of 18. He helped by walking my sister down the aisle at her wedding. My mom and I were not invited.

Another big change was that mom decided we needed to sell the house and move long distance to be closer to her brother. It was another impulsive move. My mom tended to run away from her issues, rather than deal with them. We had moved dozens of times during my childhood. But this time it was different. She dreamed of having a closer relationship with her brother. So when he casually mentioned it would be nice if she lived closer, that was all she needed. Moving was an old habit, a familiar strategy, and easy for her. However, she had yet to discover that no matter where you go, your problems come with you.

This time, we moved from our three-bedroom home into a two-bedroom apartment, and I was not happy about it. We had been in our home for the longest we'd ever been anywhere, eight years. After completing the first three challenging years of high school, I'd hoped to have an awesome final year. I looked forward to being a cool senior rather than the gawky new kid—again. My life had been going great before we moved. I had excellent friends at school, was playing 1st chair in band, and in March, the blue light had healed me. Life was good.

Moving changed everything. Making so many adjustments had been stressful. I lived in a sprawling new city, attended a huge new school, and I was socially unknown, lost among thousands of peers. Add on my new job, and new family dynamics, and I had a whole lot of new going on...

***

TONIGHT I'VE BEEN watching TV with Mom, sitting on her bed as usual. This evening, I feel odd. I'm not sure what's wrong, but I don't feel good in my gut. It's getting painfully uncomfortable, so I uncharacteristically go to my room to lie down, yet my pain and discomfort still grows. Something is really wrong. My lower abdomen is wracked with stabbing pain. This isn't the same as the appendicitis attack I had experienced while on a cruise with my mom. I had needed emergency surgery for that. This feels worse, and much more intense.

Minutes tick by, and I am trying to find a way to ease the pain. I have tried sitting and lying down, but the pain is so bad now that I can't walk or even speak! I can't even call to my mom in the next room for help. All I can manage is to throw my shoe against the closet door, which does the trick. My mom comes in, wondering at the noise and my lack of response. When she sees me writhing in pain on my bed, clutching my stomach, she runs to get a hot pad to relax whatever is going on. Then it happens...

I see a golden light that looks like flickering flames surrounding my entire body. I instantly feel warm, protected, and tingly. The pain decreases immediately. My room light is on above me. I am fully awake, my eyes are wide open, and yet I can still physically see the golden flame energy enveloping me. The golden light is really helping to ease whatever is going on with my body. I don't recall if I consciously asked for help, but I am sure my mind must have been screaming, "Help me, please!"

The light healing continues for quite a while. After the pain subsides, I stay in bed and sleep. I wake up and feel like the pain is starting again, but the golden light briefly re-appears and the pain quickly subsides. The light only fades after I am out of pain.

***

CONCLUSIONS:

I never found out what ailed me that day and have experienced nothing like it since. Something benevolent had corrected the problem and eased the pain. I had never heard of golden flame energy, so I don't really know where it came from or what brought it to me. I hadn't sensed an entity or presence. All I had seen and felt was the light... warm, healing, soothing, and calming.

Questions:

- Besides being an amazing experience, what did this mean? What was happening to me?

- Was there something or someone watching over me? Helping me when I really needed it?

- Was this a healing from God or an angel?

- What if God and angels are truly real? Could I learn to connect with them?

- Was this event meant to motivate me to continue seeking answers. another wake-up call from the universe?

Spiritual Skills Present: Clairtangency, Clairvoyance, Divine timing, Energy Healing

11

Likes & Dislikes: Random or Meaningful?

February 2, 1980, 17 yrs.

In High School, I read a book about the disappearance of the Incan civilization. It fascinated me so much that I did some research into why the population suddenly seemed to vanish. But why was this so interesting to me? Later in college, I ended up taking an archeology class about the Mayan civilization. I deciphered the Mayan glyphs so well that I was allowed to skip the final exam. I found the pyramids of the region intriguing, but I avoided delving deeply into the Aztec culture. Their apparent brutal treatment of others, the decapitations and their practices of human sacrifice appalled me.

Why have I been drawn to certain periods of history, certain cultures and languages, yet avoided some cultures and had no desire to learn more about them? Did my interests tell me something? Were they connected to memories of the past? Was it possible that I have been able to speak with certain accents because I had spoken with those accents during prior incarnations?

The oddities I'd experienced had at first felt random and quirky; but then, as time passed, I noticed that things which seemed familiar, were familiar. As my journey continued, there was almost a logic to these events. Maybe as I progressed along my path, all eventually would become clear. But before I continued my explorations, I thought it might be helpful to identify what I'm drawn to or repelled by in my current life to date. It might help with later validations.

Fascinations:

- Middle Eastern Cultures; Arabian Nights Tales

- Native American Cultures

- Science & Books

- French-Language & Culture & Fairy Tales

- The American Civil War

- Ocean and Nature

- Atlantis, Ancient Egypt, Ancient Greece

- Woodworking, Tools, the smell of wood

- Gardening, Trees

- The Inca & the Maya Cultures

- Spiritual Practices/Religions

- Classical Music, especially a few specific composers

- TV shows with magic or Time Travel

- Light and Color

<u>Things I feel very uncomfortable with</u>:

- Abhorrence of cruelty and violence

- Some religious practices

- Flushing toilets/ rushing water

- The Third Reich (The Holocaust)

- Sticky or dirty hands

- Emaciated or thin people

- Any reference to injuries to fingers or hands

** Looking at this list after moving farther along on my journey, I can see these likes and dislikes are definitely not random...

12

Speared again...

October 1, 1981, 19 yrs.

WHEN I WAS IN COLLEGE, I worked at the college bookstore. The other student workers and I had a lot of fun together, even though it had been busy at times. Since I loved books and the people who read them, it was a perfect fit. The people I worked with were great, and it was nice to have a job that adapted to my class schedule.

This incident was brief, but very vivid...

***

THIS AFTERNOON I AM behind the counter looking out through the glass doors at the front of the store when I feel the distinct sensation of being speared. It sounds crazy, but I feel a clear and painful stabbing sensation. The point enters by my low back near the spine, moves up through the left lung and then exits near the center of my chest. It happens slowly enough that I can feel it enter and exit my body, but so fast that there is no warning. All I can do is stagger to the closest chair, try to breathe, and remain calm.

What was that?! I didn't see anything. Nothing physically punctured me, but I definitely felt the sensation of a spear piercing and then pushing through my body. It was remarkably clear, which is incredible, but the pain is unpleasant.

Thank goodness, after sitting for several minutes, the discomfort subsides. My curiosity, however, is stronger than ever!

CONCLUSIONS:

It had been quite a shock to experience physical pain from an unseen object that was so distinctive I could clearly identify it. There were no outward signs that showed a physical cause of what had happened. No one was close to me in the store and clearly, there was no one around that had a spear in their hands. It was definitely not a random growing pain. It felt a little like what I'd experienced a few years ago at the antiquities museum while looking at a statue of Alexander.

I felt this stabbing sensation many more times during the years following the incident in the bookstore. The sequence was always the same. Every occurrence began as a startling surprise, accompanied by intense pain, and ending with the sensation fading away as quickly as it had begun. I was grateful it never lasted very long. But the pain was strong enough for me to have to stop whatever I was doing to try to ease it. This was one mystery I hoped to solve!

Questions:

- I'd read somewhere that all time happened simultaneously, so if that was true, could this be an echo of a traumatic event coming through from another lifetime?

- Why did it keep happening, and how can I stop it?

Spiritual Skills Present: Clairsentience, Clairtangency

13

Déjà melody

October 30, 1982, 20 yrs.

THIS INCIDENT ALSO OCCURRED while I was working at the college bookstore. I had experienced déjà vu before, but not like this...

***

PART OF MY JOB IS to arrange displays of office supplies and other gift items we sell in the bookstore. Today, I am setting up a display of some products we recently received: music boxes, statues, and other things sometimes found on knick-knack shelves. These types of things are not usually my style.

One of the items I unpack is a small, round porcelain music box. It is plain white, with an embossed scene of a water bird floating in the middle of a pond, encircled by plants and flowers. I open it to see what song it plays and immediately feel certain I know the song, though I don't consciously remember having heard it before. The label which identifies the song title is missing.

I keep listening, but still can't recall the name, even though with each replay of the tune I am more certain I know it. This feels similar to, but much stronger than déjà vu. It is more like recognizing a song without knowing where you may have heard it. Very intense feelings seem to connect to this melody;

feelings of familiarity, of profound sadness and other emotions that are difficult for me to define.

After my musical déjà vu experience, I listen to that song every time I'm at work. Eventually, I buy the music box, so I can stop hanging around the display shelves. It's evident that my intense fascination with the haunting melody is not diminishing. Even after I learn that the song is the theme from the ballet, "Swan Lake," by Tchaikovsky, I still feel a powerful uprush of feelings every time I hear it. Now, knowing the song's title, I'm guessing that the bird on the lid is supposed to be a swan.

Once I discover the composer's name, I realize that feelings have also been coming up for other music I've heard. Lately, when I listen to the classical music radio station, I notice some pieces seem familiar even when I don't know the name of them or who wrote them. The melodies are so familiar that I hum along, with no conscious memory of having heard them before. Each time this happens, the announcer comes on to say the song title and the name of the composer. Invariably, the most familiar songs are the ones written by Tchaikovsky.

Plus, there are other compositions I strongly like or dislike, without really knowing why. Why am I drawn to Borodin's works, but not to Beethoven's? Why do I like Mozart, but I can't stand Wagner? These musical preferences feel random to me, almost as random as my food preference for carrots over parsnips. However, it is becoming clear that there is something about this composer's music that feels different from all the other music I listen to.

I decide to find out more about Swan Lake and discover a sad history relating to the piece. This fascinates me since I feel a sense of sadness in response to hearing the music. When Swan Lake premiered, it was a terrible failure. They cut the ballet from four acts down to one, so it doesn't surprise me that it flopped. This devastating incident delivered a crushing blow to the young composer, both professionally and emotionally.

After I buy the music box, I figure my obsession with the song will lessen, similar to how a child's fascination with a new toy quickly fades after Christmas. But it doesn't. My enjoyment of Tchaikovsky's music continues unabated.

After this musical déjà vu, I have a startling dream involving the same melody, featuring me as a dancer in the ballet. It's the type of dream which is so realistic and detailed that I feel like I'm really alive in the dream. The vision is so remarkable that I start writing my first fictional novel, based on the scenes I experienced...

CONCLUSIONS:

The music box incident had been a strange experience for me. I had been haunted, obsessed with the song. I hadn't been able to stop thinking about it, which puzzled me. It felt weird that the music had had that effect on me. It brought up many questions that have remained unanswered. I prayed no one had seen me hanging out listening to that music box. Hopefully, my coworkers hadn't thought I was a freak.

One thing that had continued after this event was my enjoyment of Tchaikovsky's music. Listening to his beautiful songs continued to fill me with soothing contentment. But I had found it strangely coincidental how often his music played on the radio, just when I was in dire need of some calming stress relief.

Questions:

- Why did this one song have such a profound impact on me? Why had it seemed so familiar and moving?

- Why do other songs seem familiar too? Had I heard them before somewhere without realizing it?

- Why am I drawn to certain songs and composers' music styles? It seems arbitrary, but maybe it isn't.

- Perhaps my subconscious mind recognized the song (s) or maybe my intuition was trying to tell me something. I wish I knew.

Spiritual Skills Present: Clairaudience, Claircognizance, Clairempathy, Clairsentience, Intuition

14

Awake before the quake

November 20, 1982, 20 yrs.

THIS WAS A SITUATION WHERE I became aware of an event before it happened. It was of short duration, but it left a long-lasting impression...

***

I AM ASLEEP ONE NIGHT. Sound asleep. I wake up and sit bolt upright in bed. Confused, I listen and try to figure out what woke me up. After a couple of minutes, I can hear a rumbling, like thunder in the distance, which is getting closer. I hear the rumble travel from the other end of our lengthy apartment building toward me. It sounds like enormous dominoes falling... then boom! My end of the building is slammed with a jolt and I find myself in the middle of an earthquake.

The initial surge throws cassette tapes and other loose objects across my room. The sound of the wood frame building shaking is quite loud. The quake had approached like a wave from the north end of the building. Since our place is on the southern end of the building, the wave had built up power as it came toward us. It's like what happens when snapping a wet towel, the wave accelerates and rolls down through to the tip of the towel; then there is a loud crack as it snaps like a whip.

My bedroom is in the snap zone, so I feel it strongly. After the shaking stops, I check to make sure that my mom is okay. We're a bit rattled, but all good, no damage. When I asked my friends about it the next day, only a few said they noticed the quake. Most had slept right through it.

***

CONCLUSIONS:

I had been in many earthquakes since they happened fairly often in my area. But that one I remembered distinctly because somehow, I'd been roused from sleep before it arrived. If I had been asleep when it struck and the shaking had woken me up, that would have been really frightening!

Something, some sense of awareness, had awakened me before the earthquake struck. This kind of knowing something before it happened was new. Perhaps I had tuned into something outside myself. Maybe whatever had woken me up had awakened me so that I wouldn't be too scared...

Questions:

- I had heard of animals fleeing to higher ground prior to a tsunami or other natural phenomena. Was my experience similar to the instinct some animals seem to have when they sense danger?

- Was what I experienced a type of precognition? Was I reacting with an animal instinct, or was it something else?

- Had I experienced precognition or had some other force awakened me?

- How does instinct compare to intuition?

Spiritual Skills Present: Claircognizance, Intuition, Precognition

15

Brick Building with Chimneys

March 14, 1983, 20 yrs.

I'VE HAD SOME DREAMS that were so vivid that I felt like I was in another time and place. While other visions have faded from my memory almost as soon as I woke up. During the following dream, I was shown a vision so clear, and experienced such striking sensations that I'm unlikely to forget them...

I AM FLYING OVER A RIVER toward a building. The building seems to dominate the area where it is situated; on the shore, surrounded by trees and water. It is unusual, all red brick, with several tall chimneys rising high into the bright blue sky. The sun is rising on the horizon behind the building, making everything so bright it looks surreal.

The scene shifts and I find myself inside the building, walking down a long hallway lined with doors on both sides. As I peek in through each door, I see a room that has a living scene unfolding within it. I am escorted by a person or creature, shorter than me, who seems very agitated and impatient. He seems to be the custodian of this place and is eager for me to choose one of these doors and enter a room. I step into what seems to be a small room, and then find myself shooting down a natural water slide through a thick jungle! I feel the pressure of the cool water as I'm swept along in the current. I hear the roaring shush of the water and see beams of sunlight piercing through the thick canopy. Everything is so brilliant! Then the scene flips quickly back to the room, and the custodian is herding me down the hallway to the next door.

My dream adventure continues on with elaborate detail, but that's not what's most important. The building itself is the primary focus, standing three or more stories tall, its windows beaming with light. It seems almost magical. The building has a presence; it feels alive to me. Standing like a sentinel at the water's edge, the water seems to be an integral part of the building's life blood, flowing alongside and through the heart of the building.

All too soon, the dream ends, and I have to drag myself back into the present. What an incredibly vibrant experience! It's rare to have a dream that is this realistic. The building also seems very familiar. What is this dream about?

CONCLUSIONS:

In this powerful dream, I experienced events which, at first glance, seemed ordinary, like a building by a river. But because of the intense reality of the dream, I believed it meant much more. During the adventure, my attention was entirely focused on each moment as it unfolded. I had no idea what the underlying message was during the dream. Nor did I understand why the event felt so important upon awakening.

Afterwards, while recounting this incident in my journal, I recalled more of the details, which brought the dream into sharper focus. It seemed to me that dreams like these were messages from Spirit, which provided me with bits of information a little at a time. All the pieces, like a puzzle, fit together, creating a larger big picture, which eventually made sense. After some time, I noticed the messages became clear once I was ready to hear and understand them.

I had heard that dreams could be interpreted, and I knew there were books on the subject. But how should I interpret this dream? What did a building have to do with anything in my present life? I had seen every aspect of the building in such significant detail: the bricks, the windows, the chimneys, the river, and the trees. I could easily draw a picture of it. Hopefully, I would understand in time.

The images I saw looked so much like a real place that I began searching to see if what I had dreamed actually existed.

Questions:

- Is there a hidden message in this dream? Why was it so familiar and vivid? Had I been there?

- When dreams are this realistic, is part of me really there in another dimension or time?

- If I was really there, could this be an existing building, some place I could locate?

Spiritual Skills Present: Clairaudience, Claircognizance, Clairempathy, Clairsentience, Clairvoyance, Intuition

16

Synchronicity with Uncle C

November 20, 1983, 21 yrs.

THIS EVENT OCCURRED WHILE I was living with my uncle. I had transferred to a four-year College in the area and was staying with him while I was going to school. My sister and I had never spent any significant length of time with him while we were growing up. As a pilot, he was always flying, even during the holidays. His strength and authority I had found intimidating, especially since I was a shy kid. Being in charge was something he was good at after years of practice as a Captain for a major airline. "The Captain's word is Law" plaque hanging on his wall was no joke!

But after I spent more time with him playing card games like Crazy Eights and Hearts, plus his favorite backgammon variation, Acey-Deucey, I got to know him better. You can tell a lot about a person by how they play, especially challenging strategic games like those. I began to see through his armor to the really sweet guy underneath the mask. It shone through in the casual conversations we had while we were playing. Once in a while, I noticed a rare unguarded look in his eyes, a sparkle of humor, kindness, and love. He had a lot of time off and so did I.

Often, we would spend some of our free time playing video games together. That way we could hang out without really having to work at making conversation.

One of our favorite video games involved flying a plane over a scrolling landscape, dropping bombs on targets and shooting at enemy planes. It was a crude game compared to the games of today, but it was still very addicting. For the two-player game, we took turns. Player One would fly their plane until it was shot down, then Player Two would go. As with everything else, my uncle was superior at this flying game, and I sat and watched a lot while waiting for my turn. It was clear he loved to fly!

In trying to sharpen my skills so I could at least challenge him a little, I once asked him how he got so good. He said that whenever it was the other player's turn, he would practice copying what the other person did, every move and shot. I started doing this too, thinking that maybe I could sharpen my technique if I could emulate his...

***

TODAY I AM WAITING for my turn again, practicing like my uncle does, pretending to match his plane's movements on the screen, hoping to improve my chances of finally winning a game. I am excited because I am getting better at anticipating and matching his moves. He has been playing for five minutes, or maybe longer, without a mistake, and I have matched every move!

My practice ends a few moments later when I stop abruptly, feeling confused. I did not correctly anticipate my uncle's last move; the plane moved in the wrong direction. As I quickly try to get back in sync with the game, I realize my uncle has also stopped. In fact, he stopped exactly when I did. He thinks he's been practicing with me, while I think I've been practicing with him. We both think it is the other person's turn. Weird!

After we fumble with our controllers, trying to figure out whose turn it is, we discover it has actually been my turn all along. How did that happen? It's funny too, because we *both stopped* because we thought the plane should have moved the other way...

CONCLUSIONS:

Why had we both stopped at precisely the same moment? Why had we *both* thought the plane had made the wrong move? We had flown our planes for over five minutes so synchronously that neither one of us had known who was controlling the game. Then, we both stopped because we both expected the plane to move differently than it did: it zigged when it should have zagged.

It had been at that moment that I felt my uncle and I definitely had some sort of intangible connection to each other. He always seemed to anticipate my strategies, which made sense on one level given his years of practice, but it had been uncanny that he always knew what I was going to do before I did it. Every time, in every game.

The synchronous video game had really spooked me. With so many variables on the controls, it would've been a complex set of movement patterns to coordinate. For both of us to play for such a long time, flawlessly synchronized, without knowing whose turn it had been seemed inconceivable. Then, for us both to stop at the same moment, suggested to me that we were somehow sharing the same thoughts and reactions. To do that on purpose seemed impossible, unless there was some kind of connection.

After this cool experience of being in-sync, I felt I had a better understanding of the bond that twins often share. Some twins are able to sense each other's thoughts and feelings. Maybe this experience with my uncle was the same type of intuitive connection. I wonder if something exists that creates bonds between soul-mates and people in spirit families?

I'd always felt a special affinity for my uncle, a kind of unspoken comprehension, especially once I had gotten past my fear of his firm, authoritative presence. I realize now that part of my fear I had learned from my mom, who had been very intimidated by him, yet still craved his approval. Once I had released my fears, I'd been able to see him more accurately and get a glimpse of the man behind the mask. I felt I really understood a part of his essence.

Because of my relationship with my uncle, and experiencing these amazing synchronicities, I began to believe in the genuine possibility of soul-mates. He and I were so often on the same wavelength that there had to be some kind of innate communication between us, something beyond what my normal senses told me. It had happened too often for me to write it off as coincidence or random chance.

Questions:

- Is it possible for soul-mates to be family members and friends, or are they only found in romantic relationships?

Spiritual Skills Present: Claircognizance, Clairsentience, Divine timing, Intuition, Synchronicity, Telepathy

17

A Sense of Knowing

October 7, 1984, 22 yrs.

IN EARLY 1984, I got my first full-time job! I had quit college and moved in with my boyfriend, CK. He was working part-time, finishing his degree, so my new work situation brought us additional stability. There was a commute to my new job, but it wasn't too bad, especially after I started carpooling. I worked as a receptionist on a switchboard which was fairly straightforward and relatively stress-free. What was great about the job was I could do my work at the office and then, after hours, my life was my own. But soon, the job degenerated into a situation which led me to discover a new skill...

***

DURING SLOW TIMES when I complete my work and I am between phone calls, I practice typing to improve my speed and accuracy. At first I practice copying text from an old typing book, but I tire of that quickly. Then I think that if I type something interesting, maybe it will keep me practicing longer, so I start writing a novel. I got the idea for the book from a vivid ballet-themed dream I had back in 1982. Everything is going well until one day one of my managers asks me what I'm working on. I tell him I'm just practicing my typing, but he wants to see what I've written. I have no choice but to hand him the page. On it, my lead characters are sharing a touching romantic scene while practicing a ballet number. He reads it. Then, without a word, he hands it back to me and abruptly walks out of my office. Soon afterwards, my job workload increased significantly.

More work is fine with me. I enjoy being busy, but an accountant—I am not. My lack of financial savvy becomes quite clear to me when the company payroll is added to my other responsibilities. My supervisors don't seem to notice this, and not long after, I'm moved out of the reception area into the accounting department. I'm given additional duties and put to work on a computer, something for which I have no training. I feel overloaded and overwhelmed. The computer screen, with its black background and amber colored letters, is difficult to read. Because I'm staring at the screen all day, every day, I have to get glasses because of eyestrain and the headaches that come with it. My work environment and the way my boss treats me is degrading and getting worse every day. My workload has more than doubled, with no commensurate increase in pay. I feel like I need to quit, which I feel bad about because I'm not a quitter. But it doesn't matter anyway because CK has told me we can't afford to lose my salary. I have to stay.

This stressful situation continues for several more months. All I can do is pray for solutions. During quiet moments when I am alone, I sense that there is a better job coming for me soon. The new job will be more to my liking. I will earn a greater salary, and have excellent working conditions. I'm not sure why I feel this so resolutely. This kind of feeling is really odd. It doesn't seem like it's my own wishful thinking. I just know that the right job is waiting for me, and that everything will be okay. It's a strong awareness, an inner-knowing that something good is on its way, although I don't know exactly what or when. Being so off balance by the stress of my current job makes it hard to hear and listen to my inner voice. I know I need to leave this job so I can be calmer and better able to tune into the guidance that will lead me to my next job. I have a hard time convincing CK of the validity of my feelings, even though I'm certain that they are accurate. When I start coming home from work every day crying, he finally relents and agrees I should quit.

I decide to look for my next employment in the public sector rather than in the corporate arena. Never again do I want to hear, "If you don't like your job, there are 100 other people outside the door waiting to take your place." I already have feelings of self-doubt. Being told such words by the General Manager inspired me to feel undervalued and unappreciated, not inspired to work harder. I hope that if I work helping to serve the public, I will be treated better and more fairly since the focus is on service, not on profit.

Weeks pass and I have no job and no leads. I'm beginning to doubt my perceptions that a great new job is waiting for me. I apply for several county government jobs and temp agencies. I even take a qualification test with 150 other people for a city government job. Feeling desperate because nothing has panned out, I end up taking a long-term temp job to cover for a woman going on maternity leave. Before she goes on leave, she tries to train me to do her job. I usually pick up skills and information quickly, but her job is incomprehensible to me. This is demoralizing and weird. I have always excelled as a student. My self-esteem sinks lower.

After two weeks of my three-week training with her, I get a call. The city wants me to come in for a panel interview. This is unexpected, because I really had some difficulties taking their test. There were a lot of questions on it about unfamiliar subjects. I was guessing a lot and tried to follow my intuition.

On my way to the interview, I feel like I have no chance of actually getting the job, but interviewing will be good practice for me. I arrive in an excellent mood, because one of my favorite songs was playing on the radio on my way there. Because I figure I haven't got a chance, I only get a little nervous, not too much. I fumble a few of the questions they ask me, but this is practice after all. It's a good time for mistakes.

Surprisingly, I get a call the next day from the city for a second interview, during which they tell me I received one of the top scores on their test. This interview is mostly a formality to see if we will work well together. We get along fine and I get the job!

My new job consists of working with a wonderful group of people, ones that value and appreciate each other. The environment is less stressful, and there is great training in new skills, including the computer. My salary has doubled, plus I have outstanding benefits and only three phones to answer instead of thirty. What a tremendous blessing!

***

Conclusions:

My intuition about my upcoming new job had been accurate, irrefutably proven by my excellent new employment. That had shocked and amazed me. To this day, I still counted that job as one of the best jobs I've ever had in my life. I worked with remarkable people, and it had been a privilege to be part of such a fun-loving, supportive team. I also felt grateful that I'd had the opportunity to experience that kind of comradery.

Following and trusting my quiet inner voice had not been something I'd done often. Most of those subtle thoughts I had pushed aside and dismissed as coincidence. But this incident was unique. I had felt a deep sense of certainty, like contentment, or peace when thinking about being in a new job. Those feelings felt incongruent because my work situation at that time was intensely stressful, along with other parts of my life. Being so sure a new job was waiting for me, even just sensing that outcome, had been strange. Plus, realizing that I felt guided and supported had also been unusual and difficult to trust. This was the first conscious recognition of claircognizance I'd experienced in my life. I had taken a leap of faith and followed my intuitive guidance, which had resulted in me finding the perfect job when I really needed it.

Spiritual Skills Present: Claircognizance, Divine timing, Intuition, Precognition, Synchronicity

18

The Winds of Change...

August 1, 1988, 26 yrs.

THE MYSTERIOUS SPIRITUAL EVENTS which had been happening to me, had increased in number and complexity since reading that life-changing metaphysical book ten years ago. The incidents were hard for me to dismiss as coincidence, especially since they continued to happen. I hadn't noticed at the time, but the odd occurrences had dropped off a little between 1983 and 1988. The change had to be because of the influence of my partner; everything else was basically the same. I was in a relationship with CK, who had spiritual views that differed greatly from my own.

CK disapproved of metaphysics. He believed that people lived, then died, and that there was nothing more. I believed there was more to reality than what I could sense physically, and that there was some kind of spiritual continuance. I had experienced healings, which had proven to me that there was more to existence than what the five physical senses could detect. When odd spiritual events occurred, I attributed them to intuition, but he dismissed them as coincidental. To keep the peace, I'd learned not to talk about my beliefs. However, after years of unwitting suppression, I felt a deep yearning. My soul craved spiritual freedom. I hadn't realized how much I had been holding back, nor had I known how important it was for me to express my spiritual beliefs freely.

The chance to nurture my spirit self came when I discovered a mailing address in the back of that life-changing spiritual book. The author had invited readers to contact her for more information. After I finally worked up the courage, I wrote to her, and hoped for the best. My letter was a desperate attempt to connect with others who shared my beliefs. I prayed that my effort to get in touch with Anna, the book's author, would succeed. It had been 12 years since the book was published.

I was ecstatic when I received her answer to my letter, along with a copy of her current newsletter filled with articles and photos. It was proof that many others believed as I did. The most exciting part was the announcement of an upcoming metaphysical conference! There was an opportunity to meet and talk with other like-minded people, *in-person*. I wanted to go. I had to go.

The first challenge I faced in getting to this conference was convincing CK to let me go. He didn't see the value in it. But after much discussion, I suggested to him that if I went to this *one* conference, then my curiosity about metaphysics and other spiritual principles would be satisfied. Once I received answers and proof, then we could go on with our lives and there would be no more talk about metaphysics.

Another reason I felt it was important for me to go was because my Uncle Joe had passed away. He was someone I had admired and respected very much, and I was having difficulty accepting his death. I craved reassurance from people who had similar beliefs in the continuity of life and spirit. I thought the like-minded people at the Conference might relate to my spiritual views more easily than CK did. Sharing my sorrows with them might help me allay my concerns about the pain my uncle had suffered. I needed to hear what others had experienced relating to death and what came after death. I needed to *know* that my uncle was alright.

Uncle Joe was the first person in my life that truly treated me as an equal. He hadn't talked down to me like some adults talk to children. If there was something I didn't know how to do, he taught me what to do, and then he trusted me to do it. He was a well-known construction superintendent, and I worked alongside him doing home projects over the summer vacations of my youth. He trusted me to help him build a carport, dig trenches, assist with a demolition and remodel, and many other projects.

I'm sure some of my work habits came from Uncle Joe. He kept working and finished projects, even if he scraped his knuckles or got a cut and was bleeding. He worked until he finished the job. Now, I had difficulty knowing when to quit, but that was my responsibility to correct. Working hard was one thing, balancing work and life was another.

My favorite memory of him was the time we drove down to help my mom's brother (Uncle C) remodel his house. I walked in with Uncle Joe, a teenage girl carrying a sledgehammer, ready to help with the demolition. The looks I got from the other professional construction workers and my Uncle C were priceless! I felt a sense of personal power, especially when my Uncle Joe vouched for my abilities when the others questioned his decision to bring a girl to a construction site. I earned respect that day as I sledged, picked, hammered and worked as hard as any of the other guys. It wasn't my physical labor and strength that earned their respect, but my determination, perseverance and willingness to get the job done, which validated the confidence my Uncle Joe had in me. I felt far less limited by my gender after that.

My Uncle Joe died of cancer a month before the metaphysical conference. His untimely death had shocked and saddened me. He was 83 years old and had still been working when he got sick. This had been my first experience with losing a loved one whom I had grown up with. He was someone I was close to, someone who had known me. He was someone who had believed in me from the start. I had been having trouble making sense of it all. My grief over losing my uncle may have been the most convincing reason for me to go to the Conference. CK and I had finally concluded that I could go, in the hopes that I would find solace and healing.

My feelings of grief rose and fell, along with waves of anticipation and nervousness as the day of the conference drew near. Though I was a little apprehensive, because I hadn't traveled alone before, I was excited to meet people who shared my views. An uplifting and healing experience was what I wished for and what I needed the most...

***

FROM THE VERY BEGINNING, I've been excited and scared about this journey into the unknown. This is the first time I have gone to something like this by myself. I also signed up to share my hotel room, which I hope works out well. I am a little nervous about all these unfamiliar experiences.

I arrive at the airport and the first person I meet is Richard, who is a conference attendee helping to pick up other participants from the airport. He seems *very* familiar. Another déjà vu situation is cropping up again. I keep irrationally thinking his name is John. This case of déjà vu is very strong, and I really do feel I know him from somewhere.

When I arrive at check-in, I am welcomed by Justin, a gregarious, kind, and enthusiastic man; along with Joy, who has the most loving face I have ever seen on a human. I immediately feel more at ease. They tell me that to enhance our conference experience, all attendees are being requested to follow a couple of suggestions. First, we are to make a concerted effort to take part in all the conference activities. Experience has shown them that what people get out of the Conference greatly depends on what they put into it. Since I *want* to get the most out of this experience, I will definitely do my best to participate.

Their next instruction is that I should try to talk only about my beliefs, and not about subjects that usually identify who I am as a person. This means I don't share about my job, family, money, education, or where I live. They discourage any topic that is considered small talk. I think I get it. The polite but superficial conversations we have with strangers tend to keep us focused on easy, emotionally safe subjects that permit no sharing of genuine feelings, and carry no-risk of upsetting anyone. Maybe this will be helpful, especially to me, since I find these kinds of conversations challenging. If nobody can use small talk, then the playing field will be level, and I stand a chance at being able to connect with others. I *am that person* who plans what to say at parties or avoids them altogether. This could be challenging and fun!

The Conference begins, and nobody knows what to say at first. That means I'm not the only one struggling with what to say this time! It's a struggle in the beginning, but I am amazed at how quickly the veneer of politeness falls away. It feels so liberating to speak my mind without fear of being judged or rejected.

As we do activities, listen to talks, and play, I am feeling happier than I have ever felt before, able to discuss my beliefs openly with others. Throughout my childhood, I was quite shy, so it feels incredible to be comfortable talking with people about things I really care about. It is wonderful to speak freely and not worry that I am touching on forbidden topics of conversation, since no subjects are off the table. I even work up the nerve to ask Richard if we know each other from some place. He has been feeling the same déjà vu as I, but we can't figure out where or when we've met before.

I am relieved when I meet my hotel roommate, Deborah. As we get better acquainted, I discover she is very passionate and outspoken, outgoing, strong and fun. What a kick! We are getting along well and I am enjoying my experiences with her and the many new friends I am making.

The first two days of the Conference are filled with activities and speeches given by the group's leaders. The entire weekend is incredibly uplifting. So many inspiring people and encounters shine brightly in my memories from this gathering. Here are some of the events that have the greatest impact on me:

— ALBERT — is one of the presenters I get to know over the weekend. He is the most intellectual person I have ever met. He also has the strongest convictions of anyone I've interacted with. Yet, he is also one of the most kind and loving. He listens so completely and intently with his whole being as I talk with him. It is quite remarkable. His quiet, gentle strength is infectious, and he is always ready for a lively discussion, whether lighthearted or serious, a truly unique and wonderfully loving individual.

— THE TALENT SHOW — Conference attendees have signed up to share their abilities with the group in a unique Talent Show. It is an extraordinary experience for me, not only because of what happens during the show, but because I join in, despite my fear of performing. The response of the audience is joyful and heartening. They heap every performer with unflagging, unconditional, loving support. I've never seen such an enthusiastic outpouring of human kindness before. Participants risk putting themselves up in front of the entire group, just so they can share something they love to do. Skill level and/or talent seem irrelevant. It is the courage of these people that shines the brightest. They inspire me, and I feel deep admiration for them. It isn't the talent that makes the show so great; it is the amazing people, both on and off the stage. Wonderful!

One man, in particular, is incredibly uplifting. Tony makes his way to the stage, his violin in hand. He is so nervous he keeps losing his place in the piece he has memorized, so he starts over... several times. The violin is a challenging instrument to play well, and Tony is struggling. But his spirit, fortitude and perseverance are incredible and well-rewarded. With each new attempt, the Conference attendees show their support and encouragement. It is the most astonishing thing I have ever seen an audience do, providing so much loving support to a struggling performer. I am blown away by this, especially being a musician myself. I know how it feels to receive a mild response from an audience. As Tony finishes, the audience is on their feet, clapping, whistling, shouting, and many, like me, have tears streaming down their faces.

— PERFORMING IN THE TALENT SHOW — is the first time I belly dance in public. I have been taking classes, but have been too nervous and insecure about my body to perform until tonight. I do it despite my fears, so I can put maximum effort into my conference experience. I start out being so scared that I'm trembling. But by the end of the song, with such an outpouring of support from the audience, I am able to release my fears enough to actually have some fun!

— JOHNATHAN — is an older gentleman who reminds me of my Uncle Joe. We have some great conversations while sharing a time-honored conference tradition, a relaxing soak in the hotel jacuzzi. Each night, attendees fill the spa with as many people as we can fit. As I tell him about my uncle, I discover Johnathan is also a construction superintendent. Talking to Johnathan about Uncle Joe, I feel the support and understanding I hoped to find, which helps me to release my grief. His presence feels comforting, and I enjoy our conversations. We talk many times over the weekend and become good friends. His presence is a true blessing — which cannot possibly be a coincidence.

— JOY — is a lovely youthful woman who radiates loving acceptance, which she gifts to everyone along with her incredible smile. Late one evening, when just a few of us remain in the spa, Joy asks us to do something she recently tried. It's a trust activity where one person floats on their back in the water, while the rest of us lift and guide them with gentle helping hands. After the floater settles in, we sway them back and forth gently, like rocking them in a cradle. The person floating often feels a comforting sense of loving care and support. When we add the soft tones of our voices singing, "Swing Low, Sweet Chariot" this relaxing experience becomes a heartwarming gift. We all feel such peacefulness while participating in this lovely energy healing. Even participants who have a fear of water and/or trust issues say they feel much better after sharing this remarkable experience. Joy's inspiring presence is unforgettable, like an angel on Earth.

— JACKIE — is a nervous lady who is experiencing a lot of grief because of the recent passing of several friends and family members. She comes up to me after my dance performance and tells me how much she enjoyed it and adds that she strongly feels we have shared a past-life together. My dancing has brought up her past-life memories. Wow! I don't know how to respond to her, never having seen any of my past lives. I just thank her.

At the end of the Conference she invites me to come to her house and stay over for an extra night, so we can talk more. But by the end of the weekend, I feel as if I've stretched my mental, emotional, physical and spiritual selves to new limits. I sense that if I try to take in any more, or expand any further, there will be unpleasant consequences.

Upon hearing Jackie's invitation, I feel physical sensations, like energy in the center of my chest and solar plexus. It's as if I am electrically charged; it feels tingly, uncomfortable and a little painful. I decline her invitation and feel immediately relieved that tonight I'll have no other commitments but to relax and do normal things like watch TV, order room service and get some sleep. I figure if we are meant to talk more about this, there will be another opportunity.

— ANNA — is an extraordinary woman, the author of the spiritual book, which inspired me and helped me change how I perceive my world. It was Anna I wrote to, and her response which guided me here. I am definitely not disappointed. She has set aside time to talk to each individual during our last day together. The energy of her presence has made this entire weekend phenomenal. I take my turn speaking with her, sharing my deepest concerns. I'm so grateful to receive help from her and the group with my current life challenges.

Sharing on such an intimate level with people I just met two days ago has created a very close bond between us. Talking only about our honest beliefs has helped us to communicate and connect deeply on a soul level. In other settings, I have formed close ties to others, but nothing at all like this. Nothing else has ever come close to this depth, especially within so short a time frame!

The people at this conference have inspired me so much. To say I've learned a lot from being in their presence is a gross understatement. The ways we interacted with each other were challenging, but surprisingly endearing. Being part of a highly cooperative group and feeling such deep and honest connection is something I've not experienced outside of this setting. I hope I can create these types of close connections in my daily life.

For now, I have hope. There are some distinct possibilities and happier ways that we can learn to live and grow peacefully together. It's been so different getting to know these caring people. It will be a challenge to return to my life in the mainstream. Sadly, I'll probably have to go back to keeping things superficial and distant after spending this amazing time being connected and close.

I love being free to be who I really am!

***

CONCLUSIONS:

Prior to the Conference, my heart had craved closeness with like-minded people who shared my spiritual ideals. I had hoped to meet some folks who could relate to the odd things I had experienced. Thankfully, I found exactly what I'd been looking for.

Taking part in such an inspiring event had profoundly changed my life. I had met so many people of similar beliefs! There had been uplifting presenters, warm-hearted participants, plus I had met and connected with Anna. She was so down to earth. I felt very grateful for the opportunity to get to know her.

Spending time with these remarkable people had changed my ideas of how individuals and groups could interact. The intense, honest communication style we had practiced during the weekend created deep connections between us. But, I did not know how I would ever learn to talk with people in the real world in the same way. Mainstream society had repeatedly shown me it wasn't safe for me to speak with clear and direct honesty.

I had always been afraid of being my true self. Often, when I had tried to be me, I'd been rebuffed or regarded with suspicion. There were few people in my life who recognized and appreciated the real me. It had taken a great deal of effort to work up the courage to get myself to go to the conference. And when I arrived there, I had been so frightened! But when the leaders told me I would get out of the experience what I put into it, I found the strength to be vulnerable. It was time for me to step out of the shadows, time to show up for myself.

Having so many incredible conversations and experiencing challenges to my habitual beliefs had greatly expanded my perspective. I had ventured into dark corners within myself that I had never dared to go before. I had shared more of myself with others at that event than I had at any other time in my life. Being immersed in that supportive environment, I'd learned that I could be my true self. I had found the courage to face some of my fears. And because of my interactions with the encouraging participants, I had broken from my old pattern of shyness.

By the end of the weekend, all of this growth and expansion had left me with a tingling, achiness in my heart. It was almost as if the emotions that had been surging through me during the gathering had an energy to them. I felt blasted open, raw. Stepping out of my comfort zone had been exhilarating and exhausting. We had shared so much and grown so close that I would always remember this conference as the weekend I made 50 new friends!

Experiencing the beginnings of awakening had been scary, marvelous and expansive all at the same time! A few days afterwards, I realized that if I stopped seeking answers to my questions, or stopped growing, I would never be truly happy. I had to see this journey through. I had to continue. Fortunately, I would not have to continue on alone. Several of my new friends kept in touch with me after the conference and continued being a part of my life.

For that weekend at least, I had gone from being a shy, disconnected, lost person to one who easily connected with many people! The joy that came from the connections, the understanding, and the camaraderie was something I'd never felt before. From that point forward, I decided to seek people who wanted to create deep connections; people who supported each other's growth and evolution.

I also hope to witness someday the dissipation of the divisive influences that have been so prevalent in our world. I long for the day when people can effortlessly and deeply connect to each other and experience the joy of being seen and heard as their true selves.

Spiritual Skills Present: Claircognizance, Clairempathy, Clairsentience, Clairtangency, Divine timing, Energy Healing, Intuition, Retrocognition, Synchronicity

19

Richard! Richard!

September 7, 1988, 26 yrs.

AFTER THE CONFERENCE, I went to visit my grandma and dad before returning home. I always stayed with my grandma in her cozy condo. She and her place were the only things that were consistently dependable and stable through my childhood years into adulthood. I had many happy memories associated with her and her home. She was my sanctuary.

Grandma and I had always gotten along exceptionally well together. She often said we had a special relationship, a connection that was unusually close. She was very religious and was always being of service in some capacity to her church or community. We would talk about her religion, but she had never forced her beliefs on me. She respected me and my beliefs, as I respected hers. She was the person I could say just about anything to, without fear of censure or judgment, and I was so excited to share what I had experienced at the conference with her...

***

IT IS MY FIRST NIGHT with Grandma after the conference, and I tell her all about it. She is enthusiastic as I describe in detail my likes and dislikes, my joys and fears, and my doubts and elations. We talk for a long time before she goes to bed, then I journal, read and go to sleep too. I fall asleep very quickly, especially since I am exhausted from staying up late every night at the conference.

I sleep well at my grandma's house, probably because I feel safe in this loving environment and because the same little twin bed has been here for me since I was a child. My dreams here also seem to be plentiful and sweet, possibly due to the nearness of the ocean, but most likely because of the radiance of my grandmother's love. Tonight, my dreams seem more lively than usual.

In my most vivid dream, I am actually in a scene from one of my favorite old movies. I am distraught and can hear my voice repeatedly screaming, "Richard! Richard!" It is such an agonizing experience. I wake up still urgently calling out that name. I am thoroughly shaken.

In the movie, the other main character successfully travels back in time. He goes to the past to find his soulmate where they meet and fall in love. Near the end of the movie, he accidentally returns to the future. As he is swept forward in time, his love is left behind; trapped in the past. She reaches out and repeatedly screams his name as she tries to stop him from being taken away.

In my dream, I am the woman who is abruptly parted from her soul mate after being ecstatically reunited with him. Tragically, they are forever apart, and she is alone for the rest of her lifetime.

My voice screaming Richard's name is what I hear in my dream. I am screaming with the same sense of desperation, the same expression of panic and despair. Awakening out of breath, wildly glancing around the room, searching but not finding, I am desolate. Did the woman who was left behind feel such complete devastation and loneliness? My heart aches with a deep sorrow from which tears cannot flow. It takes a long while to shake the emotions evoked by this dream.

***

CONCLUSIONS:

The intense feelings brought up by the dream continued through that day and beyond. I was miserable when I thought about how I would've felt if I'd found my true love and then had been forcibly separated from them again. Why had this startling vision brought up such powerful feelings of longing and sadness? Had the dream meant something more than the replay of a movie scene?

Perhaps the strange connection to Richard I'd experienced at the conference and this dream were somehow related. We had only just met for the first time, yet I felt a strong familiarity. I had felt that déjà vu feeling again, like I had sensed at other times in my life. Only this time it had been different. The feelings were so compelling that I had asked him if we'd met before; I even asked if his name was John, a name that repeatedly came to mind whenever I saw him. He had had similar feelings of recognition and was drawn to me as well. I sincerely hoped that someday these mysteries would be solved.

Questions:

- Does this dream somehow connect to the person I met at the Conference?

- How can people seem so familiar when there is no way we could have met in this lifetime?

- I have had several occurrences of déjà vu in my life. What do they mean?

Spiritual Skills Present: Claircognizance, Clairempathy, Clairsentience, Intuition

20

Past Life Reading #1

April 19, 1989, 26 yrs.

THE 1988 CONFERENCE had changed my life. The personal connections, the loving acceptance, and the support I had received, was something that, prior to the Conference, I had only read about. I had grown so much from the experience. My perspective had changed and had broadened to encompass more viewpoints. I was now closer to accepting, as valid, all those strange events which had been happening to me. I could not keep dismissing my experiences as imagination.

The friendships that had begun at the Conference continued into my *real* life. These relationships helped me remember what I'd experienced and helped me to keep the faith. They reminded me I hadn't dreamed the experience. I was determined to continue on the spiritual journey I had begun. But honestly, I didn't know what to do next.

I had read my spiritual book several times to keep myself inspired and hopeful. I'd noticed that the people in the book used several tools to accelerate their spiritual development. They progressed with the support of their mentors and from interacting with other evolved friends. They also challenged themselves to step out of their comfort zone by trying new things and taking risks. If they made mistakes, they didn't wallow in self-recriminations. They took the opportunity to learn from the results of their choices. The characters also experienced exceptionally rapid spiritual growth by reviewing some of their past lives with the help of a special playback device.

With these tools and support, they were able to discover and resolve some of the past behavior patterns that connected to the present. These repeated patterns revealed several lessons that had not been mastered. Facing their issues had helped them to broaden their perspective and develop spiritually. Their present life challenges provided clues as to what lessons were left undone. Being reminded of this process prompted me to consider something similar. Perhaps the time had come for me to get out of my comfort zone and delve into my past.

Unlike the characters in the book, I had no supportive community. I was surrounded by naysayers and skeptics. Therefore, daily interactions with spiritually evolved people were not a possibility at the time. Nor was there a machine which could access my subconscious mind and provide me with a simple way to review my past lifetimes. I needed to reveal the hidden memories of my former lives, if they really existed, in a way that would be accurate and believable. If there was a way, then I would also need proof that what had been retrieved was real and not some creative figments of imagination.

I decided to seek professional help. I'd heard of intuitives, who had the ability to see, hear, and sense things beyond the physical realm. It seemed they had access to information that I could not tune into. I had inquired at the metaphysical bookstore and found there was a someone available who could do a past life reading for me. I was told that she had intuitive abilities which would enable her to see into my prior lifetimes. Perhaps, with her help, I would finally get some answers...

***

I AM NERVOUS. I have spoken with very few psychics, and so far, I'm not sure I can trust their perceptions. After watching several of them do readings at psychic fairs, I've noticed that the information some intuitives relay is vague and often based on details gathered by observing the client or by asking them questions. I want to be able to verify what I am told by this person. I really want to believe.

I go in. We talk for a bit. She asks what I do for a living, what my beliefs are, and some other information about me. I tell her I work for the government, a little about my family and of my involvement with friends from the spiritual conference.

Then she gets quiet and describes bits of several lifetimes. I sit quietly, watch her, and listen to her descriptions.

The first past life she describes is one in Atlantis, where I start out as a female temple healer. Later in that life, I work for a government office which reviews and approves highly advanced technological devices. While investigating the viability of some proposed devices, I discover some shady stuff and earn quick advancement along with the wrath of the shady developers of these devices. That life ends with me being assassinated. She tells me that some of my friends that I met at the conference in the present were coworkers in that lifetime. She adds that we have come back to help heal others and the Earth.

The next life she describes is in Egypt where, again, I am a government worker (male this time). My job is tallying the crops that farmers bring in to the central granaries. She says I am working in this position when I meet my current life partner. He is a farmer. We become friends, more than friends, and that we have had several lifetimes together. She also mentions that we respect each other's work, "a mutual job respect thing."

In the third and final lifetime, she describes me as being in the position of a Burgermeister, a mayor of a small town in Germany very long ago, in yet another government job. She says I am a large, bearded, jovial man, whose cheerful wife is my present-day mother and my happy little daughter is my present-day sister. We form a close knit family group.

I am well-liked and do a decent job as mayor. After several years in office, I want to improve the opportunities for the spiritual growth of my citizens. I hire a troop of performers to enact Bible stories in German. My wish is that it will make it easier for people to understand the lessons in the Bible. I want it to be more memorable for my people, something they can enjoy more than a solemn Latin mass.

The plays are successful in helping to uplift my people and guide them forward on the path of spiritual development. The psychic says that my efforts don't go unnoticed. The plays continue to gain popularity, and in time, come to be known as the "German Reformation Movement." She says that many of the people who were influenced by these performances are now part of the new-age movement. Some of them are my spiritual friends.

***

CONCLUSIONS:

This had been an interesting experience, but I questioned the validity of it. I was skeptical of her findings because it seemed like she based her stories on the information I had provided to her. My current job, my new friends, and details about family members were all things I had told her about before the reading began. Was it possible that she used all the information I had given her to create a perfect explanation of my present life circumstances in a one-hour session?

It had been strange that all the lifetimes she related had one element in common, that I worked for the government in some capacity, like my current employment. Had it been a coincidence or had she taken what I had told her and embellished it?

Some events and locations felt right. I had long been interested in Atlantis and Egypt, but not Germany. Her account, regardless of the series of events, seemed to generally describe me as a person. She'd also alluded to my deep-seated beliefs about wanting to help others, which was true. But I think we had talked about both subjects before the session.

Though there seemed to be some validity in what she said, it was of no use to me because I could not verify the information she had provided. There was no internet to help me do my research. My resources were libraries and bookstores. Information about Atlantis and Egypt was particularly difficult to find. The books I had dug up were based on conjecture and theories about Atlantis. Egyptian texts included general historical events, not specific descriptions of the daily lives of regular people. There were no individual histories with accurate details in the library, or any place I had access to.

Maybe it hadn't been a good idea to pursue this. Exploring my past would not help me progress unless I could get reliable, verifiable information. I also needed to know how my past life lessons connected to my present life challenges.

The most important thing I had decided as a result of getting this reading done was that if I was meant to receive knowledge and insights from my past-lives, then I needed to see it for myself.

Questions:

- Why had I worked for the government if every life she saw?

- The psychic had tapped into three lifetimes that included most of my immediate family and friends—could that be true? And if so, how am I to verify this?

- How much of what a psychic perceives is distorted because they bring what they sense through their own consciousness?

- What if having someone tell me about my past is like when several eyewitnesses to an accident each describe a different version of what happened? Are all the versions true from a certain point of view?

- Will I ever be able to get clear, reliable information if it comes through someone else besides me?

Spiritual Skills Present: Claircognizance, Clairsentience, Clairvoyance, Retrocognition

Section Two – Disbelief to Possibility

So many things have happened now that

I can no longer be comfortable in

my disbelief.

In my search for answers, I've had some astonishing,

life-changing, first-hand experiences.

I have been asking for proof, and

I am receiving it.

Can this possibly be real?

21

Opening my Eyes...

August 27, 1989, 27 yrs.

AT THE 1988 METAPHYSICAL CONFERENCE, I had begun several close friendships, and in the year that followed, I stayed in touch with many of the people I'd met. It had been a joyful surprise that it was easy to maintain these connections! I had not foreseen the profound effect the Conference would have on my life.

My assumption that I could go to such an event in order to get it out of my system had been quite naïve. After all that I'd experienced, there was no way I would allow myself to lose my new friends and their amazing, expansive, spiritual support. My partner CK wouldn't like it, but I had to go to the next conference. My spirit self encouraged me to continue my association with these people, my heart longed for it, and my self-respect demanded it. I explained my conclusions to CK and asked that he support my spiritual growth, as I have always supported his.

Two of my new friends and I had kept in very close contact. We hoped to see each other soon at the next conference. But during the '88 Conference, we had heard people talking about an amazing spiritual destination that was located nearby. It was only a short drive from where the '89 Conference was being held. After talking about it for months, Deborah, Robert, and

I decided we wanted to take a side trip to that special place together, and then attend the conference afterwards. We had fun planning our journey and hoped to see and experience some amazing things.

Besides enjoying the stunning views, the trails, and the splendid rock formations, we planned to explore the town and visit some of the inspirational shops. Most importantly, we wanted to experience the energy vortexes. These energetic hot spots had reportedly helped many people to accelerate their spiritual awakening. There was a lot to discover, so we planned to be there for several days before the conference. I hoped five days would be enough to see all that we wanted to see...

It is Day One of our trip. We meet at the airport, which will be the starting point of our 5-day journey. We stop along the way to see some beautiful cliff-dwellings. Carved into chalky white stone, the structures stand high above the ground, the remnants of an ancient settlement. The bright whiteness of the indigenous rock here is a startling contrast to the sandy brown landscape we drove through to get here. Sycamore trees, which have a sweet smell, thrive in the area by the creek, along with cicadas whose music fills the air. The lush trees and undergrowth differ from the surrounding flat, arid expanse, making this place feel like an oasis. Walking in the footsteps of the ancient peoples who had lived out their daily lives here, I can almost sense the presence of the people themselves. This echo of human residents I think I have also felt at other historic sites.

We get back on the road, eager to get to our ultimate destination, and are surprised to witness the surroundings rapidly changing to a landscape of vivid rust-colored rock. As we come into the area, sandstone formations of all shapes and sizes surround us, including tall buttes, flat-topped mesas and canyons that are too breathtaking to be described with words. The contrast of the brightly colored spires against the blue sky and white clouds seems too lovely to be real. We are all excited to be here.

We check into our hotel and quickly head to the nearest spiritual bookshop. We want more information about the vortexes nearby. This area is known to have many of these energetic hotspots, which are said to emanate concentrations of positive and negative earth energies. It is this energy which is supposed to help people to expand their psychic senses and assist with spiritual awakenings. We want to know how to get to these energy centers as soon as possible, in order to see what effect they might have on us.

The first vortex we go to is near the top of a high, flat mesa. We park overlooking some of the magnificent buttes named for their distinctive shapes. My friends and I meditate for a while. I'm waiting to feel the energies, hoping to sense something (ready, set... go!). But nothing happens—not for any of us.

We decide to go back to some of the other vortexes and formations that we passed on our drive through town. Unfortunately, we experience the same results and resign ourselves to a quiet evening back at the hotel. However, when a magnificent land formation suddenly comes into view, we decide we definitely need to stop one more time. The trail to climb up the tall butte is open to the public, and we can see people hiking on trails near its peak. We don't want to miss an opportunity to get closer to the extraordinary beauty of one of these natural marvels. Surrounded by these ancient structures, imagining the time and circumstances which created them, I am awestruck.

Leaving our car in the lot near the road, we follow the trail into the area. As we get closer, I begin to feel what seems like energy. It's as if there is static electricity in the air. Now and then I see tiny sparks of light, like the kind I see when I stand up too fast. I keep watching and walking. I'm not light-headed or dizzy. But the closer we get, the more discomfort I feel in my heart and solar plexus. There is a sharp pressure, similar to what I sensed after the 1988 conference when I was so psychically blasted open. Back then, I assumed the pain was telling me I was overloaded and that I couldn't handle any more. Now, feeling this again, I am not sure what the sensation means. Am I getting overwhelmed by the energy?

Is it harmful? Am I ill? Are my energy centers opening and should it be painful, or does this pain have some kind of meaning? What does it signify and how am I supposed to handle it? The pain makes me think twice about going any closer today. We have already flown, driven, and stopped at several places. Maybe I need to relax and have some quiet time. I am feeling like I'm not ready to face whatever is bringing up this pain. I tell my friends of my discomfort and we decide to come back in the morning when we are more refreshed and it is cooler. It is very hot and dry here in August.

DAY TWO. We come back to climb the butte in the cool mid-morning. The pressure in my chest and gut starts again when we arrive, but now it's a warm, tingling sensation of energy, which is tolerable. I meditate on the rocks after our climb. We have each stopped at a height we are comfortable with. My meditation is nice, but not the incredible awakening I keep hoping the vortex energy will initiate.

As we drive back toward our hotel after spending several hours climbing the butte. We see a sign indicating a turnoff to a small chapel which overlooks this magnificent valley. We decide to check it out. I love the sacred atmosphere of churches. It sounds especially cool and peaceful, perfect after our hike, which we finished in the afternoon heat.

We walk up to the entrance and discover that they made the chapel out of the same red rock that is indigenous to this area. Since the Chapel is located on a slight rise, there is an expansive view of the valley floor, surrounded by the magnificent towering buttes. It surprised us to discover that a famous architect designed this non-denominational chapel. The building is tall and rectangular; solid rock walls on two sides, with glass on the front and back ends. The support structure that holds the glass is shaped like an enormous stone cross. I go in and stand at the back wall and look toward the altar out the windows. The glass wall allows visitors to see an incredible vista of red buttes, green and brown flat lands stretching into infinity, with bright blue skies beyond. I marvel at the beauty of this setting.

Within the chapel, we each find ourselves a place to relax. I choose to sit in a back corner, away from everyone. They have Gregorian chant music on, which seems haunting, familiar and strangely comforting as it echoes off the stone walls. There are small candles burning in the front, near the altar, giving off a subtly sweet, sacred aroma. The simple wooden pews stand silently in rows, offering support. In the dim coolness beneath the stone ceiling, the atmosphere created here is perfect for prayer and meditation.

I look at the unadorned, enormous stone cross, and then close my eyes. Because I'm afraid of being interrupted while in a state of deep reflection, I don't actually try to meditate in such a public place. I just relax, let go of all my cares, and enjoy the music and the atmosphere of the sacred space...

+++

I'm not sure how long I have been sitting here when I start seeing and hearing myself in a different place and time. It is almost like I am asleep and dreaming, but I am definitely awake. It is raining in this scene. I hear crying and see a crowd of people on a hilltop. I am stunned when I look up from the body I am in. I see three crosses on the top of the hill, with men attached to them. I hear a voice, soft and gentle, saying hello, letting me know he is there. It is definitely not my voice, definitely male—I have experienced nothing like this before. I feel vulnerable and alone, something I usually only feel at night. But with the scene before me, and the emotions I'm experiencing, I am very frightened right now. Yet, reassurance and serenity emanate from the voice. It is a comforting sound. He tells me his name is Achaeus, and that he is my spirit guide.

The scene continues, and I become aware of where I am and what is happening. Looking down at my body, I see the clothing of a Roman soldier, leather sandals on my feet. I am at the Crucifixion of Christ. With horror, I realize that I helped put these men on their crosses. The overwhelming sense that this is decidedly wrong feels like an up-rushing wave of emotions, a terrible inner conflict. I was following orders; I had to. But now I'm feeling like I should disobey, even risk punishment or death. I cannot accept that I allowed myself to be a part of this. Tears of agony flow down my face. I want to stop this event from happening somehow... keep it from continuing.

But then, through the haze of my emotional turmoil, I hear another voice reach me. It is a unique voice—deeper, calmer, wiser, and distinctively different from the first voice. I feel a deep sense of peace envelop me, a presence so profound and loving that I know, somehow, who it is. It is Him, the Master of Light, the Son of God, Jesus Himself, who asks me,

"What do you wish to know? What answers do you seek?"

What is happening to me!? I am astonished at sensing His peaceful presence. This is amazing! And yet, I am in a panic. How can I decide at a moment's notice which question to ask? Of all my many questions, which one should I ask? Which question do I need answered most? What an incredible opportunity! What if I ask the wrong one?

After a few moments of gathering my thoughts from the shock of hearing Him speak directly to me, I decide to ask,

"Why must there be pain in the world?" thinking of my emotional pain and the agonies He is suffering on the cross.

He says, "It is necessary."

I say, "But why?"

He says, "Because pain is an excellent teacher."

His answer seems so simple and obvious. It feels reassuring, yet, for an answer to come directly from Source, it seems too easy. I feel some doubt rise within me.

His voice calms me in the Chapel, but the part of me who is a Roman soldier is in emotional agony. I am experiencing the soldier's feelings about this situation, trapped by duty, trained to follow orders. But at this moment, I strongly feel that it is a horrible, cruel act, and it feels so real to me right now, standing at the foot of that cross. The cries of the people swirl around

me, and rain falls like teardrops on my skin. I know that that
soldier is me. I helped to crucify Christ. How do I live with this
knowledge?

The soft tones of Achaeus' kind voice come through again.
He is checking on me, comforting me. I sense that the other
presence is no longer here. Slowly, my awareness shifts and I
become more cognizant of where I am, in the chapel, in my own
body, and in the present. I am no longer the soldier on a rainy
hilltop. I am me, sitting here in the little chapel. Tears running
unchecked down my face. I had helped put Jesus on the cross!
Oh my God! What did I just experience? Was it another life—a
past life? As the soldier, I could see and feel my body. I felt the
mud; and I heard the rain and the despairing cries of the people
echoing around me. I was there. It was so real; so real that I
blame myself... Could I have stopped it, or made any difference?

+++

I take a while to stop crying and pull myself together. I have no
idea how long this encounter has been going on, or how much
time has passed. Still shaken, I don't see my friends inside, so I
step out into the brightness of the setting sun. I see my friends
waiting, just as bewildered as I am, both with tears on their
faces. It turns out they also experienced something deeply
moving, yet none of us feel able to share our experiences.
We are all so overwhelmed that we can't find words which
could sufficiently convey what we saw and heard. Yet, we all
agree that our time in this little chapel has been powerful,
life-changing and beyond anything we might have imagined.
What an amazing gift of experience!

As I go through the rest of my day, I keep checking to see
if Achaeus, my spirit guide, is still with me. He is, and he
continues to be near, his gentle voice never far, always patient

in responding to my endless questions. I verify his presence often, hoping that he is real, fearful that he's not. The more I listen to his voice, the more I begin to believe that he is really there.

Now that I can sense he is with me, I do not feel alone anymore. It is an enormous relief to not feel so isolated, disconnected and afraid. I suppose I haven't ever been as alone as I thought I was.

***

CONCLUSIONS:

My friends and I discovered later that week that the Chapel was actually considered an energy vortex. That had been a surprise, but one that made perfect sense. We each had desperately wanted to experience something extraordinary during our visit, and Spirit had guided us to the best place to have that experience.

After what happened in the Chapel, I'd realized that when we went to the first vortex, I had expected to sense something, but hadn't known what. My fear of the unknown may have gotten in the way. After all the time and effort we had invested in setting up our trip, I'd been worried that *nothing* would happen. There had also been the possibility that *something* would actually happen, which was also a little scary. In the end, I believed that my anxious thoughts had kept me from experiencing anything that first day. Our expansive experiences had finally occurred when we relaxed and stopped getting in our own way.

When we had stopped at the Chapel, we'd only been seeking a cool place to rest. We had no other expectations. Relaxing and dropping our guard had allowed us to receive what we had really come for. We had all been surprised.

One of the biggest surprises for me had been the gentle quiet of Jesus' voice. I'd been accustomed to hearing the sound of my own thoughts, much like my voice, swirling in my mind. But male voices, distinctly different from my own, the sound of Achaeus and Jesus, had not been the voices I'd expected. I had assumed that such high spiritual beings might have spoken with startling, earth-shaking voices. Perhaps that had been something I'd seen in the movies. With Jesus, what I had actually experienced was subtle, so gentle, and easy. Had it not been for the vivid emotions, the visions and the intense presence that had preceded his voice, I might have not noticed His gentle murmurings. The sense of being embraced in peace beyond measure had been the most convincing factor. All of my anxiety had stilled, and instead I'd been filled with acceptance and love.

I thought about the answer to my question about pain which I received in the Chapel. I had to admit that pain had driven me to make realizations and helped me to learn needed lessons many times in my life. Whenever I had missed the gentle whispers from Spirit which came first, pain inevitably followed and got my attention. Sometimes, the pain needed to increase significantly for me to take notice and take action. But in the end, pain had often forced me to reevaluate my choices and make necessary changes.

This experience changed my life. From the enormity of the events I had witnessed in the chapel, to the constant companionship of my spirit guide Achaeus, my life path has been undeniably, wondrously altered.

I had asked to see things for myself after my past life reading in April. The information the intuitive reader had relayed to me, a second hand interpretation about my past lives, had been interesting but this was immeasurably better. Experiencing things first hand, the sights and sounds, the powerful presences, noticing my own reactions to the events I witnessed, had been a much more potent experience. I had seen and sensed things for myself!

I suppose these incredible experiences would not have happened if I hadn't been ready for the burden of truth. The information that came through was hard to accept and hard to live with. I don't know how my friends dealt with what they saw and felt. We could never fully talk about what we each experienced. But for me, despite the upsetting information, I had become more aware of energies and beings that I had not been able to sense before. With each experience, it was becoming easier to believe. I knew now that we were not alone...

Spiritual Skills Present: Clairalience, Clairaudience, Claircognizance, Clairempathy, Clairsentience, Clairtangency, Clairvoyance, Divine timing, Intuition, Meditation, Retrocognition, Telepathy

22

"I am the Gentle Breeze..."

August 29, 1989, 27 yrs.

DAY THREE OF OUR TRIP brought more surprises. My friends and I had had some remarkable experiences at the chapel the day before. The visions, the emotions, the sensations in my body, and the voices I'd heard had been a lot to take in. These interactions had been so overwhelming that by the next day, I had begun to have doubts about their validity. I decided I needed to ask for proof...

SINCE LEAVING THE CHAPEL yesterday, I have been checking in with Achaeus, my guide, every so often just to see if he is still there, like a young child who keeps checking to see if their parent is close at hand.

"Are you there?" I ask in my mind.

"Yes. I'm here." I hear Achaeus answer.

When my friends and I stop to do another meditation out near the rocks, I ask Achaeus again if he is really there. Is he truly real? Am I actually sensing something or do I just have a fertile imagination? His voice is so quiet and subtle.

I finally ask him, "Is there some physical way for me to know for sure?"

He replies, "Yes. I am still with you... I am in the gentle breeze that caresses your face."

The funny thing is, is that there has been absolutely no breeze on this hot dry day until I hear his reply, then a gentle wisp of wind touches my face, then stops as his words fade away.

Surprised, I ask several more times over the next few days, just to test it, to see if the wind is a fluke or random coincidence. I ask my questions and a touch of breeze accompanies every reply. How wondrous and strange!

CONCLUSIONS:

Many people would call what I experienced a coincidence. But at what point do we recognize such synchronicities are not random? How many coincidental events had to happen to me before I realized that what I'd sensed was something real? The situation had been so odd. I had asked my questions while sweltering in the breezeless desert heat, and yet when each answer came, it was simultaneously accompanied by a cool breeze. I had asked many questions, yet during the silences and while I was asking my questions, there was no air movement at all. It happened the same way every time. The cool wind only came when I heard my guide's answers. Weird.

These coincidences reminded me of a sci-fi show I saw where a ship and its crew were caught in a repeating loop of time and were reliving the same day over and over again. It wasn't until after they noticed hundreds of coincidental events that they realized the events were not accidental; they were clues. Once they had recognized this, they'd been able to free themselves. Was I in a similar trap? Maybe I needed to take these subtle intuitive clues more seriously so that I could find solutions to the problems that had me feeling trapped.

If what had happened during my trip was real, then perhaps things were more connected than I had previously thought.

Questions:

- Will my messages and lessons keep repeating until I can no longer ignore them?

- Do I receive messages subconsciously to guide me because I cannot sense them consciously?

- Will the coincidences keep increasing in frequency until I am able to sense them somehow?

- Who is sending these messages, and are they from a reliable, trustworthy source?

- Can my thoughts or the thoughts of Spirit alter my physical reality?

Spiritual Skills Present: Clairaudience, Clairsentience, Clairtangency

23

Ants!

August 30, 1989, 27 yrs.

BY DAY FOUR of our trip, I had experienced so many life-changing events! I was surprised and grateful that I could still sense the presence of my spirit guide, Achaeus. To be in direct communication with him was extraordinary.

Our trip had provided many opportunities for wonder and growth, and we still had two days left to explore! On this day, we sought another vortex deep at the end of a canyon trail. By the end of the trail, we found more than just trees, energy and scenic beauty...

***

WE'VE BEEN ENJOYING exploring many of the natural and man-made sites that are plentiful in the area, but our goal is to visit all the vortexes while we are here. My friends and I decide to hike the long canyon trail so that we can get to the vortex located deep in the canyon, near the end of the trail. Other people we have met during our visit have strongly recommended it. We prepare for our hike by loading our packs with provisions and water, and set out early in the morning.

The tall sandstone walls tower above us as we make our way down the trail. The colors of the buttes constantly change as the sun moves, and the greenery flowing over the top and cascading down sides of the bright sandstone walls seems mystical and reminds me of Atlantis. I'm not sure why.

Up ahead, we see a cave high above the trail at the edge of one of the buttes. There is a steep path leading to it, which we climb so we can get a closer look. From this high perch, we can see out into the canyon. It is a beautiful view, but what makes it even more special is the energetic presence of the indigenous people who were living here centuries before our arrival. I wonder if it was difficult living in this rugged but remarkably beautiful environment. There are signs of habitation throughout the cave, from wall foundations to the holes in the slabs of rock left from preparing food.

We continue on the trail, which becomes less civilized the further we go. My friends walk on ahead, while I stop to take pictures. I see dozens of large red ants bustling in and out of large anthills. These ants have a painful, stinging bite.

As I watch in fascination, images suddenly flash through my mind. I see a man in a blue Union soldier's uniform. He is an unkind, cruel man, who treats native peoples with vicious contempt. He has been captured, and is being treated to his just rewards, tied naked, face down to anthills like these and left to die from the sun, the heat and the ants. Suddenly, I realize this man was me. I feel an emotional rush of self-loathing and disgust in response to discovering the kind of man I had been: selfish, greedy, and filthy in mind, body, and spirit.

The vision stops just as quickly as it began. I walk on, trying to clear my mind and heart of the images, and trying to release my feelings of strong dislike toward this man (myself), and my revulsion at seeing the way he died. It is hard to shake these creepy feelings.

I hurry to catch up with my friends who are up ahead of me. Winding our way through this peaceful canyon surrounded by the dappled sunlight, the tall trees and the red striated rocks towering into the bright blue sky, I feel awestruck and small. I am like a tiny spark of life compared to the majesty of nature. This setting helps me gain perspective, release some of my feelings and not be overcome by what I just experienced.

We come to a clearing where someone has constructed a medicine wheel near a dry riverbed. The energy in this canyon is so peaceful that no one on the trail speaks above a hushed tone. It is like being in nature's church, and we are on sacred ground.

Even the trees are energized and I can feel their benevolent wisdom, and how they and the earth are in balance. I am reminded of a movie in which the lead character has a wise advisor who is a tree spirit, an ancient mother of trees. I find such a tree near the end of the trail and feel comforted by its presence.

We stop at a secluded spot in what we believe is the vortex and meditate. I am able to soak up the peaceful energy, but don't experience any additional visions. After our pleasant break and lunch, we make our way back out of the canyon to return to civilization. While walking past the anthills, I still feel a twinge of discomfort. I hurry by, distracting myself by talking with my friends and getting lost in the scenic wonders around me. As we return to the start of the trail, at the mouth of the canyon, I feel a little sad. I am reluctant to be leaving this inspiring and peaceful setting. I hope to return someday and walk the trails of this beautiful canyon once again.

***

CONCLUSIONS:

What had been happening with these visions? Had some type of spiritual door opened within me, or was there something about this place? What I had seen of the Union soldier's experience was intense, but could it have been just my imagination replaying a movie scene from a western? I don't recall watching anything like that; yet it had been so clear, the rush of feelings, the disgust, and the sudden knowledge that that soldier was me. It had nearly overpowered me, and I had felt the need to distance myself from that spot. It was like I was watching it from outside, but also feeling and thinking what he was thinking from inside of him. What a strange and scary event.

I had felt so much. Waves of pain emanated from the tortured soldier. I had felt disgust at suddenly knowing his thoughts, his cruelty and his twisted enjoyment in causing other beings pain. I felt ashamed, recognizing that he had been a part of me. The worst was feeling his primal fears, intensified by memories which flashed through his mind, earlier traumas rising to the surface because of his impending death.

The journey on the trail had brought up harsh revelations. But the magnificent energy of the canyon had overpowered most of the trauma. There are some visions you never forget. I had witnessed such beauty...the trail winding through majestic trees; white puffy clouds floating in blue skies; and the stunning red buttes rising like ancient sentinels. My eyes had beheld nature's spectacular showcase, and more.

Later, back at the hotel room, I'd journaled and processed what I had experienced that day, and still, I couldn't fathom why it had happened. It was so strange to have sensed that connection or past life scene with the soldier near the start of the canyon trail. I started looking at the books we'd bought to try to focus my thoughts on more pleasant things. After skimming a book about vortexes, I uncovered a clue… they considered the entire canyon to be a concentrated energy vortex!

Questions:

- Why did that soldier death scene pop into my mind?

- Did being in these vortexes amplify memories or something else?

- Were the vortexes enhancing my intuitive abilities?

- Were my visions connected to lessons I still needed to learn?

Spiritual Skills Present: Clairaudience, Claircognizance, Clairempathy, Clairsentience, Clairtangency, Clairvoyance, Retrocognition

24

Meditation Rocks and Achaeus...

August 31, 1989, 27 yrs.

BY DAY FIVE, the final day of our trip, my friends and I had seen and experienced a great deal. The last thing we wanted to do before we returned to the big city was to go meditate one more time among the rocks. Every day, we had gone out to various rock formations to meditate, sometimes in the morning or at sunset, and a few times when millions of stars filled the sky. Each place had its own special magic.

For me, it had been three days since the appearance of my spirit guide Achaeus. His steady, reliable presence, the breeze, and the information he had told me made it easier to believe that he was real. On this last day, I had decided to trust him enough to ask for more specific advice...

I HAVE BEEN HEARING that the vortex energies not only amplify the spiritual senses, but can also heighten emotions, too. I am experiencing both. Emotional tensions are running high between my friends and I, we all seem to be feeling overly sensitive. Maybe it is because we have all had spiritually expanding experiences and sometimes rapid changes can be uncomfortable and overwhelming. I am also preoccupied with my own life challenges and current feelings of stress. My relationship with my partner, CK, is part of my inner turmoil. Things are not as harmonious as I expected they would be, and I am trying to decide how to help the situation. Should I try to heal things if possible, or will it be better to let it go?

I have been asking my guide questions about simple subjects, ones that I can verify easily. But now that I feel a growing sense of trust that I am communicating with a higher source of wisdom and not just talking to myself, maybe I can ask about more serious and personal topics. I don't fully understand this communication yet, but I feel more certain about the reliability of his advice. I decide to ask him, "What do I do about my current relationship? Should I stay or should I leave?"

Achaeus' clear answer is that I should stay and take care of CK. During our conversation about this, I also get the distinct impression that he knows me and CK very well, and that we have known each other since ancient times. This communication is very specific, and I am surprised and delighted by the clarity. It is hard to convey how it feels to be able to trust and feel supported by Spirit. I am so grateful to sense his spiritual presence and support.

***

CONCLUSIONS:

My interaction with Achaeus was remarkable and marked an important beginning. I followed his advice, which had been in alignment with my thoughts. I wanted to make every possible effort to save my relationship with CK rather than just quit and leave. After I received such strong, supportive advice from Achaeus, I believed I would receive help from Spirit with my decision to stay.

The week here with my friends had gone both fast and slow. We had all enjoyed our trip, and it had been an eventful one. I'd had some amazing experiences and delighted in the incredible beauty and atmosphere of the area. But there had been challenges too, and I was ready to return to town and go to the metaphysical conference.

I had felt increasingly emotionally fragile as each day passed, and by the end of the week, I was overwhelmed. I did not know how I would handle the intensity and challenges of the conference in that condition. It had been a beautiful, scary and amazing trip. The scenery, the spiritual presences, and the heart opening I'd experienced had all been life altering. The pain I'd felt in my solar plexus when I had arrived was gone and in its place was a warm, tingly, expanding sense of energy, connection and peace. It had been one of the most incredible weeks of my life!

It would take time to come to terms with what I'd experienced in the chapel, seeing and hearing Jesus and being a Roman soldier.

Before this trip, I had often felt different and sometimes I felt like an odd person, but I had always felt alone. Beneath my feelings of loneliness and separation was the fear that I would always be alone, not worthy of loving relationships with people who valued my presence in their lives. But having met my spirit guide, Achaeus, and having the gift of his wisdom was something that I valued beyond measure. With his steadfast presence, I felt valued; I felt worthy, and I would never feel alone and isolated again.

Questions:

- Will I still be able to sense my guide when I return home after my trip?

Spiritual Skills Present: Clairaudience, Claircognizance, Clairtangency, Clairvoyance, Divine timing, Energy Healing, Retrocognition

25

Metaphysical Conference '89...

September 1, 1989, 27 yrs.

My FRIENDS AND I completed our side trip to the vortexes and headed back to the city to attend our second metaphysical conference. The journey had been awe-inspiring, but it would take me a while to process all that had happened. However, processing would have to wait, because there were three days of Conference fun yet to experience.

At this second Conference, I initially felt more at ease. After we arrived, I was delighted to get the chance to renew some friendships I had begun last year. It would also be good to meet new people and participate in activities that were less intense than what I had just experienced. I hoped this conference would be amazing, like the first one, but in different ways...

***

I AM SO HAPPY TO be greeted by some of the friends I made last year. I'm also looking forward to seeing Richard again. He seemed so familiar to me when I met him at the first conference, but I never figured out why we felt such strong déjà vu. This time I would like to spend more time with him to see if we can solve that puzzle, plus he is fun to hang out with. When I find him it seems like he was looking for me too, along with

Justin, another person I met last year who I also wanted to be better friends with. Now we are having fun planning a hilarious act for the annual talent show, laughing hysterically and being incredibly silly. I love it! It feels wonderful to have friends that I can drop my guard and be serious or playful with.

The most important part of the conference for me this year are the interactions with the people, having fun being with new and old friends. I feel much more confident. I am seeing a new side of myself, one less fearful than before.

The experiences of our trip are still haunting me, and I feel uprushes of many emotions, like guilt, elation, doubt and fear. I feel guilty over what I did in my past life, elation at meeting my guide and JC, doubt in myself and my perceptions, and fear that it didn't really happen or that it did really happen. There are some tensions which remain between me and the friends I went on the trip with, but that is something that I can't change or fix in my current state of being. I am already feeling spiritually overwhelmed, and the conference has only just begun.

I am happy to spend more time with Anna. I feel like she told us before that she is not very intuitive, but somehow when it is my turn to chat with her individually she knows that I have just had a life-altering experience, and she even seems to know the details of it. How can this be? This astonishes me, but I also find it to be reassuring. If she can somehow sense what I saw and felt, even part of it, then maybe it was real and I should stop having doubts about my experience and my sanity.

During the Conference, the communication with my guide continues, which is incredible and still surprises me. But now, things are different. I am different, and how I perceive myself and my role in the world is different. I have connected with...a piece of eternity. I don't understand it yet. I'm having difficulty believing all that has happened, and yet, I feel expanded, as if I am more than I was before. Maybe I have always been this way, but just couldn't sense it until now.

***

CONCLUSIONS:

I felt uplifted after the second Conference, as much as I had after the first one, but in different ways. Unlike last year, I had begun the Conference already spiritually blasted open. Perhaps what I'd needed most this year was the fun and relaxing time I'd spent with friends. The fact that Anna had known about my life-changing experience was the icing on the cake, the best highlight of all. Her validation of my vision was exactly what I needed at that moment.

Many of the friendships which had begun last year, especially with Richard and Justin, had deepened over the course of the Conference. I felt blessed to have such wonderful friends who seemed so familiar and awesome.

Most important, the communication and closeness of my spirit guide had continued, even down here in the city, away from the beautiful rocks, valleys and buttes. This gave me hope that the life-altering changes I had experienced there were going to continue when I got home!

Questions:

- How are people connected besides the conventional five senses? I hope to one day understand how this is possible, and how it works.

- Will I still be able to sense my spirit guide when I return home?

Spiritual Skills Present: Clairaudience, Claircognizance, Clairempathy, Clairsentience, Retrocognition

26

Who Said That?

September 7, 1989, 27 yrs.

AFTER THE CONFERENCE ended, I was eager to go some place
familiar and comfortable so I could slow down and regain my
equilibrium. All the experiences I'd had during the vortex trip
before the Conference were still a confused jumble in my mind.
I hadn't had time to sort it all out. Grandma's house was the best
place to let my guard down and write about my adventures...

I AM BACK AT GRANDMA'S house for rest, relaxation, and recovery. I
tell her a lot about my trip and the conference. What I don't tell
her is my vision of the rainy hillside, the Roman soldier, or my
brief conversation with Jesus. I still feel guilty for my role in that
life, if a lifetime is what I truly saw. My grandma is very loving
and is a spiritual and religious person. I don't know how she will
feel about some of my experiences, but I tell her most of it. I can
always count on her to listen to me, whether she agrees with
what I'm saying or not. She values what I have to say and listens
with an open mind. Even the metaphysical concepts I share
with her, ideas she probably doesn't agree with, she listens to
with respect for my beliefs. She is wonderfully awesome.

My morning wake-ups here are usually very slow, stretching, enjoying the secure comfort of my tiny childhood bed in this loving environment. This particular morning, for some reason, I am quickly wide awake. I sit up and swing my legs to the floor, then I hear it, a clear voice saying,

"Can I be your child?"

I glance quickly around the room. I heard it so clearly; it sounds like the voice came from inside this room.

"What?!" I say aloud.

The voice says again, "Can I be your baby?"

The feelings that rush up when I hear this question are joyful. I feel uplifted and I say, "Sure!"

***

CONCLUSIONS:

This is one experience I had not told Grandma about. Since it had been such a clear voice that I'd heard, with the message twice repeated, I believed it to be real; otherwise, I would have thought I was still dreaming. It also seemed believable to me because a friend of mine told me a year ago that this had happened to her.

This happened in September. By October I was pregnant, which was incredible because CK and I had been trying for several months to conceive. Weird and amazing.

This conversation with the spirit of the child was not the last; it was the first of many. These conversations continued throughout the pregnancy. If I was ever upset or crying, the baby would kick like crazy, and I would feel nauseous. It was like the baby and I were so in tune that if I was upset, the baby would get upset as well. I didn't know how to start a conversation with the baby, so I asked about its gender. It seemed like a male voice responded. Later on, the voice said that if he were a boy, then he would leave me and go create his own life and family and be gone more. If she were a girl, even if she married and had her own family, I would be more included in her family. She also promised to take care of me as we both got older.

It ended up that I was blessed with a beautiful daughter, and we have remained as close as ever.

Spiritual Skills Present: Clairaudience, Clairtangency, Precognition

27

Still with me...

October 30, 1989, 27 yrs.

THE VIVID ADVENTURES I'd experienced during my vortex trip felt larger than life while I was having them. It was like I had been living a dream which I would awaken from when I returned to my real life. I'd been afraid that the memories of my wondrous experiences would fade, and in time, I would doubt that they really happened. Thankfully, Spirit had other plans...

***

MY PARTNER CK'S CHURCH services are not given in English but in his language, which I don't speak very well. Nevertheless, I enjoy going there because I love the sacred feel of churches. Recently, I have realized that some of the church rituals, like the smell of the candles, the smoky frankincense, the colorful windows, the feel of the wooden pews, and the hushed environment, are uplifting and comforting to me.

After being so close to nature during our excursion into red rock country, feeling my spirit guides' presence with me while I was outside, and feeling the wind on my face, it seems odd to be indoors in a beautiful, but formal church setting. I don't try to follow what they are saying, I just allow the musical tones of the language to wash over me. My eyes drift closed and I go into a meditative state.

Soon, I feel a peaceful presence envelop me, similar to what I felt in the chapel during my trip to the vortexes. It is a very comforting feeling. I have been stressed about some current life challenges. I hear the same distinct voice, the gentle, loving words in answer to my unspoken concerns, and feel the touch of His hand, warm and gentle on my arm. It is so physically tangible and real. I am very relieved and comforted. I did not realize how afraid I was that what happened on my vacation was not real. I was also worried that I would have to be there, among the energy vortexes, to feel that kind of spiritual support, afraid I would not feel it at home. Being able to sense the beautiful spiritual presence of Jesus again now, I feel profoundly relieved and blessed.

I am so grateful that I can sense the presence of Spirit and feel his encouragement in the here and now. Maybe this means that I can be anywhere and still feel supported by Spirit. Amazing spiritual experiences are not location dependent... how wonderful is that!

I didn't dream it! It is real.

***

CONCLUSIONS:

My experiences while visiting the energy vortexes had been amazing. But they had also been very challenging, a little frightening and difficult to come to terms with. My greatest concern had been that the communication and closeness I had felt during my trip would disappear once I got home. After I felt

Jesus' (JC) presence with me in my local church, I had hope that my ability to sense Spirit would continue to develop. I had been worried that I had to have the energy boost of the vortexes to sense anything. This occasion made it seem possible that my connections might become something more enduring.

More importantly, JC's presence and his answers to my questions showed me that he did not blame me or hold me responsible for his death because of my actions as a Roman soldier. This was the most relieving thing he could have told me, since I had still been feeling deeply upset about that.

This brief, but powerful encounter helped me to start bridging the gap between my theoretical beliefs and my daily life. As I used what I had learned from my spiritual experiences to improve my everyday actions, the experiences were validated and my quality of life was enhanced. I was beginning to understand the importance of learning from my past. I could see clues in my current habits that showed me lessons I still needed to work on.

It also seemed crucial that I consider carefully what I did with the knowledge that I had gained. I felt that any knowledge that could not be applied to my daily life remained a collection of facts in my head. However, if I used my new beliefs, thoughts, and knowledge to transform some of my life's challenges, then I had the potential to develop wisdom.

Spiritual Skills Present: Clairaudience, Claircognizance, Clairempathy, Clairsentience, Clairtangency

28

Spiritual Retreat 1991

September 1, 1991, 29 yrs.

THE OPPORTUNITY TO ENJOY the life changing spiritual conference weekends had come to an end in 1990. Anna had been organizing them for a long time and was ready to do something else. My disappointment was keenly felt; these annual gatherings had been such a crucial source of inspiration, connection and transformation. Knowing I wouldn't be able to meet with my soul-sustaining friends was devastating. I felt like I had finally found my people, and now we would be parted from each other.

Thank goodness a few dedicated members stepped forward and put together a Spiritual Retreat. We gathered together once again, this time at a beautiful conference center nestled high in the majestic mountains. I'd hoped that connecting with my spiritual friends would be as uplifting as it had been at prior conferences.

I looked forward to the inspiring presentations, the shared music and laughter, and a hilarious new talent show. There was also going to be a guided group meditation, which I was also eager to try. I hadn't done very much meditating and hoped I would be able to tune in. Often, when I'd tried on my own, my mind had been so active that I'd had trouble following the directions. I wanted to relax, and stay focused on connecting to spirit...

***

ONE OF THE SPEAKERS IS leading the group in a musical meditation. We are gathered in a circle in a large room at the hotel. It is lovely music, a relaxing meditation, and the energy of the group is wonderfully powerful. For Jackie, one of the ladies I met in 1988, it becomes too much. She is upset and crying. Several people move close to support her and assist with healing. I am one of them. Jackie has been drawn to me since the very first conference, when she told me that she knew me before in another lifetime. She wanted to talk with me more after that first Conference, but I could not talk to her about it at the time because I was feeling so overwhelmed.

Today is different, and I am at her side trying to lend my loving support. As soon as I draw near to her, a scene from our shared lifetime appears in my mind's eye. We are both in the ancient past. Both of us are part of a harem. I have been in the harem for a while and know how to navigate the social intrigues relating to that lifestyle. I am a long-time favorite, while she is a very young new arrival. Girls are often brought here, whether they were bought or kidnapped, and forced into this stressful life.

Jackie is crying in the scene from the past I'm viewing. She has been selected to visit the sultan tonight. She is young and inexperienced and terrified that she will displease him. Often, girls do not return from such a visit, especially if the sultan is unhappy, and I am concerned for her life. I am trying to talk with her and console her as best I can.

I hear my thoughts repeating over and over in my head, "She's so young, so young..."

I decide to go instead of her. She feels bad and doesn't want me to take her place, but I choose to go.

I never return.

The vision fades as I return to the present, and the meditation is still going on. Something feels different. The situation in the room feels lighter and continues to brighten. It felt heavy and somehow darker before. When the room feels more relaxed and peaceful, and Jackie gets quieter, it's as if the situation is healed and resolution is felt by all. People begin to disperse, and Jackie grows calmer. As the music fades out, I'm wondering what Jackie was experiencing and if she saw any of the same events I did. After the session is over, Jackie, her husband and I agree to meet later for lunch to talk about what happened.

When I arrive at the restaurant, I discover them already waiting. Jackie sits, hands fluttering, face anxious, nervously wondering what I experienced. Without preamble, I turn to her and say,

"It was my choice."

She clearly understands what I am referring to, and her tears begin to fall again. She still feels guilty. We each talk about what we experienced, both then and now, and our stories match up exactly. The only differences are in our perspectives. It is uncanny.

My belly dancing performance in the talent show at the 1988 Conference had stirred her memory. She remembered our previous life together, but we hadn't spoken of it, and I hadn't retrieved it until today. She has been dealing with this, and the loss of several family members in her present life for years. After we talk, it is clear by her face and body language that the weight of guilt has lifted from her and she is much more at peace. We hug and when I leave; she is smiling, sincerely smiling.

***

CONCLUSIONS:

This absolutely could not have been a coincidence! We had each remembered the same past life scenes. We had tuned in separately, and yet we both had clear understandings of the emotions and conversations we'd shared. We were both drawn to the same scene, the same traumatic moment, without ever having talked about it beforehand. Yet, our stories matched exactly! Could it have really happened?

The circumstances of how this event had been unfolded to us both were so strange. It hadn't occurred to me how rare an event this had been until I had written it down. It had been centuries since these events had occurred, yet the strength of the feelings that arose had been undeniable. Jackie felt guilty about my death in this past life and was haunted by it centuries later. She had been deeply affected by her remembrance of this lifetime. A few years ago, I had been similarly overwhelmed by feelings of guilt when flashbacks of me as a Roman soldier had flooded in. How could feelings remain so strong after so much time had passed?

Perhaps the concept I'd heard, which described time as something less constant and more fluid, provided a plausible explanation. If time didn't flow in a straight line, but was constantly in motion in a continuous loop, that would change things. It would mean that all the events of the past were still in motion. If all lifetimes were happening at the same time, then perhaps our memories remain strong because they are still playing out. Maybe the feelings that had come up at the retreat were vivid because they were still taking place and were still unresolved. Jackie had not released her feelings of guilt until I had shared the insights I'd seen with her. Tuning into the big picture, putting another piece of the puzzle into place, had brought clarity and relief to us both.

Maybe the threads of unresolved thoughts and feelings stayed alive and present in some part of our souls. I wasn't sure how the puzzle of time and space and spirit all fit together. Perhaps the conscious mind was mainly focused on the present location, rather than bouncing back into memories from other times. But if some part of consciousness or soul allowed these memories to bubble up from the past, it would explain why some of my visions and feelings had been so clear and strong, and how they could still affect me in the present. In a way, these feelings, these connections to the past, were a gift. Maybe they gave me chances to come to terms with the past and be free of it. Maybe they gave me opportunities to release old traumas and heal in the present.

Questions:

- How was it possible that both of us saw, sensed, and described the same events with no other outside person directing the recall process?

- This regression had happened spontaneously, involving both of us. Could the fact that it happened that way be considered some kind of validation?

Spiritual Skills Present: Clairaudience, Claircognizance, Clairempathy, Clairsentience, Clairvoyance, Intuition, Retrocognition, Synchronicity

29

Vivid Dream...or?

March 13, 1992, 29 yrs.

I HAD GONE WITH my baby daughter to visit my grandma. We'd been having a relaxing and fun stay as we usually did. Every minute spent with grandma was a joy for me, and now my daughter was also enjoying her loving presence.

After we'd had a tiring day, I settled down for some quiet time with Grandma, after I had put my baby down to sleep. After Grandma went to bed, I decided to stay out on the living room couch so I wouldn't wake the baby...

***

WHILE I AM ASLEEP, I experience another vibrant dream. I am in a large log cabin, surrounded by trees and greenery. The author of the past lives books I've been reading is here with me. We are carrying on a lively conversation. He is wearing a light blue shirt and I can see and feel myself walking around inside the cabin. The details are extraordinary; it is so lifelike. I can smell the wood, the forest, sense the textures—I feel like I'm really there.

I suddenly hear my baby start crying, and I am yanked out of the dream. I open my eyes but can't move my body. It's as if I am not fully here. My dream self seems to be separate from my physical body. I panic a little and then try to think of what to do to solve this dilemma.

I have an idea. Maybe it is intuition, wishful thinking, or even something I saw in a movie, but I give it a try. I visualize an image of my energetic self sitting down in my body and laying back, fully stretching out into my physical form in an attempt to merge my spirit body back together with my physical one. I see my energetic body disappear into the physical body on the couch, and in an instant, the two rejoined.

I'm surprised at how abruptly it happens, but I can feel that I am definitely back in my physical body. The weird thing is, I still can't move! It feels as though I'm entirely encased in a shell of heavy lead or metal. I try to lift my arm and can't.

Slowly, as I focus my mind, I gain more strength and am able to move my arm, which falls limply off the couch. My struggle continues until, after some time, I can sit. I am feeling frustrated and anxious because I am still trying to get to my crying child, yet I am having trouble controlling my muscles. I try to stand, but fall back onto the couch on my first attempt, dizzy and disoriented. Eventually, I am able to hobble my way down the hall to reach my baby.

It is a while before my physical body responds easily to my thoughts again, and even though it is responding, my body feels extremely heavy to me now. I crave the energetic lightness I was feeling before.

***

Conclusions:

This had been an intense adventure. What had happened to me could be described as an out-of-body experience. I had read just a little about astral travel prior to that event. The idea of traveling around in my spirit body, freed from the limits of my physical self, had a lot of appeal. According to what I read, some people knew how to will their spirit body to step out of their physical one. Guided meditations had been designed to help people learn these techniques. I had tried to do this a few times, but had been unsuccessful.

What surprised me most about this incident was that my physical body had turned out to be so heavy and dense. The sensation of going from a light and responsive body to a leaden and stifled one was so incredibly traumatic. That sensation I will never forget.

I had never seriously attempted to leave my body, and this occurrence had not been consciously done. But after this experience, I made no further attempts to do astral projection. The trauma of re-entry into the dense physical body was much too difficult to deal with. It was not worth it.

After this experience, several things became evident. This event proved to me that the spirit or astral body could leave the physical body and return unharmed. When my spirit body returned, I had been disoriented for a short time, but otherwise my physical body was fine. The process of returning had helped me to understand, in a very dramatic way, that the physical realm was composed of heavy, dense matter.

The journey had also shown that there was a place beyond the physical dimension. I had powerful recollections of where I had been, what I'd done, and memories of carrying on vibrant discussions with others. My inner self, my memory and ways of thinking were unchanged while I was in my spirit body. The contrast between being in a spirit body versus being in a physical body had been so strong, it was clear to me that there are states of being beyond the physical dimension.

It amazed me that such an ordinary day could turn into an unforgettable one, just by going to sleep.

Questions:

- Were the Spirit body and physical body connected or sustained in some way even when separated?

Spiritual Skills Present: Astral Projection/Out of Body, Clairalience, Clairaudience, Clairtangency, Clairvoyance, Intuition

30

Local Spiritual Experience

May 24, 1992, 29 yrs.

IN 1992, AFTER A YEAR FULL of challenges (aka learning opportunities), I'd felt the need for some help with accepting some of my lessons. While searching, I had found out that there were classes and spiritual meetings I could attend being offered at a nearby metaphysical bookstore. I decided to check it out and get a book at the same time...

***

ON THE DAY I GO to the bookstore, there is a lecture about metaphysics being given by some local practitioners. I am hoping the lecture is about how the past can influence the present. As it happens, they are talking about past lives today. They are also doing a demonstration. The facilitator, with the help of a clairvoyant, will bring people up from the audience to show how their regression process works.

I really want help today with my current emotional traumas, and want to prove to myself that it is possible for me to remember my past lives, and not just when I'm in the vortex zone. I desperately hope they pick me. They tell the audience members not to raise their hands, that the facilitator and the clairvoyant will make the selection. After a minute or two of scanning the audience, the facilitator picks someone near the front and turns to the clairvoyant for confirmation.

The clairvoyant looks straight at me and says,

"No, her," as he points in my direction.

I am delighted and shocked, happy and frightened.

The facilitator asks, "Are you sure?"

The clairvoyant replies, "It's got to be her."

Gathering my courage, I leave my safe spot in the back of the room and make my way forward. I am stunned that I got picked. I have often hoped to be the winner of a drawing, or to be summoned from the audience. But this is the first time I sincerely wished to be selected, and it happened!

I'm glad to be chosen, though being up in front of a room full of strangers is discomforting, to say the least. The lights feel like spotlights on my face, and I am nervous. After a brief meditative induction, the clairvoyant describes a scene. I can imagine parts of what he describes, and I'm surprised by a strong uprush of feelings, which they tell me is a sign that I'm tuning into something accurate. I'm shocked by the unfolding events and start to feel a little overwhelmed as they guide me through this deeply personal experience. During my brief time up front, I receive help with what troubles me most, my personal life and the recent end of my relationship with CK.

Afterwards, shaken, tears on my face, I head back to my seat. There are other demonstrations going on, but my mind is in a whirl. I am distracted by what I just experienced. I feel I should investigate this further, find something or someone to help me access my past so I can see it for myself.

On the way out of the store, I search for the book I came in to purchase. Not seeing it on the shelves, I go to the front counter where people are browsing and ask the clerk if they have a book on aura colors.

Another customer overhears my question and says without missing a beat, "Your aura is green."

Not catching on, I explain to her that, "I'm looking for a book about aura colors."

"Well, it's green just the same," she says.

I am surprised to realize she can actually see my aura! Since most of the aura photos I've had taken show a large cloud of bright green light around me, I believe her. I wonder what it would be like to have the ability to see the glowing swirls of energies that surround people.

This day is turning out to be full of surprises!

CONCLUSIONS:

On that adventurous day, I'd experienced three important things that greatly affected my future.

First, the book I purchased had inspired a significant amount of self-acceptance and understanding. Second, when that woman described my aura without prompting or using any kind of special camera, it had been a spontaneous, authentic verification. I had wondered many times if people could actually see auras, now I need wonder no more. Third, when I'd been chosen by the clairvoyant, it seemed like he had heard my plea. He and the facilitator had helped me to tune into my past intentionally, and being able to do that was a significant change.

So far in my life, traumatic scenes from the past had popped in unexpectedly. These had been helpful for my growth, but sometimes the timing had been inconvenient. If I could tune into the past at times of my own choosing, or find people who could guide me, it might accelerate my journey. If I asked Spirit to help me discover past-life answers to issues that were still impacting me in the present, perhaps I could resolve specific problems. I longed to free myself from the traumas which were holding me back and keeping me in fear.

After the events of the day, I went straight home to sign up for the Past-Life Regression seminar that was being held on my birthday. I was determined to learn how to revisit my own past-lives!

Spiritual Skills Present: Auras, Clairaudience, Clairsentience, Clairvoyance, Divine timing, Retrocognition, Telepathy

31

Past-Life Regression Seminar

July 20, 1992, 29 yrs.

AFTER MY FIRST PAST-LIFE READING in April 1989, I had realized I wanted to see things for myself without depending on someone else's interpretation. I'd also wanted to receive detailed, accurate, and verifiable information. Later that year, I got what I had asked for in the chapel vortex, when I'd been able to view, firsthand, part of my life as a Roman soldier. That experience had been so much more intense than receiving a reading. Personal contact with Spirit had changed my life.

Several incidents had occurred since my vortex trip. It was as if a door had cracked open, and spiritual energies and information about the past had started slipping through. My communication with Spirit had grown in small ways, little by little. My spirit guide and I connected regularly, and I no longer felt isolated and alone. There had been a definite increase in both the number and the intensity of spontaneous intuitive events in my life.

I believed that if I could find a way to intentionally discover patterns repeating from my past lives, then perhaps the knowledge gained would help me come to terms with some of my present life challenges. If I could learn to see a bigger picture, how events connected, then I might more readily comprehend and accept that the situations in my life have had a purpose. Thus far, some parts of my life had made no sense and felt very unfair. I also wanted to feel more certain that the soul continues after the body dies. It would be a great relief to no longer fear death.

I had read a few books about past lives and tried some meditation tapes created by the same author. Listening to the meditations had helped me relax since I'd been feeling stressed and fearful because of current life challenges. I found my tension lessening doing them, because I was able to go into a deep state of relaxation from his words and the sound of his voice. It was supposed to be self-hypnosis, but it never seemed like it hypnotized me. I felt calmer and able to focus on what the words were telling me to visualize. I felt very safe doing these, and they helped me de-stress a lot.

I had been using every tool I'd learned to help me deal with the fear, grief and anxiety that I had experienced since my breakup with CK. But there were still times, especially while trying to sleep at night, when primal fears arose and sent my imagination spinning through an endless series of horrible what-if's. It can be so challenging when relationships end!

When I discovered that the author of the books and meditations would be teaching a past-life regression seminar near the energy vortexes on my birthday, I was ecstatic. It had to be a sign from the universe that I needed to attend. Fortunately, I got my wish...

***

I ARRIVE AT THE AIRPORT and journey up to my hotel near the vortex zone just before a summer storm opens up. Later that night, I am blessed to witness a spectacular showcase of nature's fireworks: sheet lightning across the distant mountains accompanied by the music of the pouring rain. The powerful storm causes flash flooding, which freaks me out, but I cannot help but watch the beauty of it. Though I enjoy watching, I am worried about being able to get to the seminar tomorrow and hope the roads will be clear and NOT what they are now: fast flowing muddy rivers cutting across the land.

The next day, I awaken to clear blue skies filled with puffy white clouds. The roads are clear, and I arrive at the seminar without incident. After brief introductions and talk about their own spiritual journeys, our hosts, Jack and Amelia, begin the seminar.

We start by learning about how to do automatic writing and then practice trying to read our fellow participants. This intuitive technique is a way of allowing my higher self or another spirit to write using my hand. I'm not very good at it, maybe because I'm afraid to let something else be in control of my hand. The fear of the unknown has me a little apprehensive. I'm also not sure what to do since I've not heard of this technique before. I get a little info about the person I read, but it feels like I made it up. The person reading me gets more information, but it seems to be rather generalized and vague. My primary concern is, how do I know who will take control of my hand?

We move on to the next activity, our first past-life regression. Jack describes how we will proceed. He'll begin with a meditation where he guides us through a relaxing visualization, and then he will lead us into a hypnotic state. Jack says that many people ignore the suggestions made during hypnosis and do whatever they feel like doing, which is okay. He emphasizes that people do NOT do things while hypnotized, that they wouldn't do fully awake. In other words, I can't be forced to perform some embarrassing trick while I'm in a trance, and then wake up to discover I have no knowledge of my performance.

This information reassures me, since it disproves what I've seen portrayed in the media. I'm glad to know that hypnotists can't make people do crazy things without their knowledge and consent. Hypnosis is a relaxing technique which has helped me through some troubled times, and I'm relieved to know for sure it's safe.

After being reassured that we each have control of ourselves and our experience, I feel better, a lot better. I can relax and trust the process now that I know hypnosis is a calm state of hyper-focus. Next, to prepare us for our past-life journey, participants spread out into all areas of the room, and get comfortable.

Jack begins the past-life meditation, describing natural settings with a soothing voice to help us go deeper into a calm state of relaxation. To guide us to the past, we imagine walking through a dark tunnel toward a light, and then stepping out into a prior life. I go through and exit the tunnel, and find myself in the midst of a vivid past life memory.

+++

I LOOK DOWN AT MY FEET and see that I have square-toed boots on. As my gaze drifts upward, I discover I am a Spanish soldier, wearing a helmet and armor on my upper body. I sense that I am on a mission for the Queen.

My boots grind on the flat stones of a high plateau as I walk toward the open expanse of an unexpected canyon, which blocks our progress. I'm so pre-occupied with searching the rocky canyon for a passable trail that I don't notice how close I am to the edge. Caught unawares, I lose my footing and tumble into the canyon. Somehow, I manage to grab the edge of the cliff and cling to the side. I call for help and hear footsteps approach. It is a comrade of mine, a fellow soldier. He looks at me, but makes no move to help. In his eyes, I can see a venomous look of hatred; he has no intention of helping me at all.

While dangling from the side of the rocky cliff, I hear a quiet voice inside me say, "Let go, I'm your angel. I will take care of you. It will be okay." I don't let go.

My muscles are tiring, and I beg for help from my comrade. He tells me, "Let go!"

Even though I'm feeling desperate, I still don't let go. Suddenly, without warning, he draws his sword and brings it down toward the ledge, severing my hands from my body.

Now I am falling down into the deep canyon. The first thing my body hits is a ledge which was below me, out of my range of vision, but having no hands, I cannot grasp anything to stop myself from continuing to fall.

Bruised and battered, I end up at the bottom of the cliff, lying face up. I can see my comrade. He picks up my hands and throws them down on top of me. This is the last thing I see in that lifetime.

As that life fades, I realize two things. First, if I had trusted my inner voice, wherever it came from and whoever it was, I would have been all right, as the voice had promised. I could have grabbed that ledge and climbed to safety. Second, even though my Spanish comrade looked a lot different, I know the man who cut off my hands was my former partner, CK, the one I'd just broken up with in my present life.

+++

Jack ends the activity and then pauses for us to ask questions. When I am called on, I describe what I have seen and then ask, "How do I know I didn't just make it up or imagine what I saw?"

He says many people think they imagine things,

"However," he says, "Why would anyone choose to imagine those particular scenes and bring up those specific memories?"

He has a good point. His follow up is perfect,

"If you were to make it all up, why not make up a wonderful life of fame, fortune and happily ever after, rather than despair, betrayal, self-loathing, disfigurement and death?"

The next thing we do is an activity where we meet all of our inner selves and listen to what they want to tell us. This is an interesting way of communicating with aspects of my higher self and I get excellent advice, such as, "Don't judge yourself so harshly," "Cut yourself some slack," and "Take care of me." My child-self asks that I play, really let go and do things with no other purpose in mind, with no distractions, so we can have some real fun. This exercise helps me identify a fear of letting go, a fear of violence, a distaste for watching people get hurt, and a fear of being alone.

In the next meditation, we follow a path which leads to a special protected place that has a book which holds the wisdom of my life. My book is open to a particular page which has this written on it:

"There is a balance of truth, beauty and wisdom present in all things; only take the time to observe, listen, and appreciate, and you will see them."

After I receive that wonderful advice, I am told to walk along various pathways where I receive additional insights. Guided meditation seems to be an easy and relaxing way to help me learn to focus and get in touch with higher wisdom. I am really enjoying this type of meditation, where my mind is directed to do something. I have been told before that the best meditation practice is to think of a blank wall and clear my mind of all thoughts, which had never worked for me. My mind does not naturally quiet down. But now that I see there are many types of meditation, I can look for methods that will work for me.

In the next meditation, they ask us to visualize ourselves walking down a path in a natural setting. This is easy for me because I was walking the canyon trail yesterday and can easily recreate what I saw on that beautiful journey. I see myself walking in the shade with tiny spotlights of sunshine beaming through the trees. I hear the gentle sounds of nature, smell the cedar and pines, sense the earth beneath my feet, and relax into an expanding inner stillness.

I am directed to visualize my higher self, and soon, a tall nymph-like being wearing a diaphanous flowing dress appears in my mind's eye. Together, we continue on the path until we come to a clearing where stairs lead up to the sky. My higher self and I seem to be the same being now, and I run up the stairs and leap into the starry sky. I fly to a place I am told to create, a special space, a sanctuary for my spirit self. With my thoughts, I create a beautiful place, floating amongst the stars, a lovely blending of structure and function, water and stone, plants, and air. I am told to design everything exactly the way I want it, making any desired changes with a thought. Redecorating has never been so easy!

I am told to ask my spirit guide to come in for a visit. I do this and Achaeus arrives. We sit together and have a long talk. I am able to ask many questions, get answers and receive his wise counsel. This is such a wonderful way to connect with him. I am surprised at how quickly the answers come flowing in. The meditation ends too quickly, but I know I will definitely do this again at home.

The last activity of the seminar is an in-depth past-life regression. They guide the group into a relaxed state through visualizations and then lead us into the past through a door at the end of a tunnel. Every time I do this, it becomes easier. With each practice, I am becoming more familiar with my own responses, and I am learning to trust them more.

+++

THIS TIME, WHEN I ARRIVE IN THE PAST, I see myself as a clean-cut young man, tall and blonde. I am hiking down a mountain trail, surrounded by verdant green meadows, grey peaks and a scattering of trees. I am wearing dark green shorts which have embroidered straps to hold them up. I have a pack on my back, and I am coming into town for supplies. I seem happy, adventurous, and full of fun and vigor.

I am told to skip to the next big event in my life. I see myself very clearly in a large, beautiful church standing near the front altar, watching a veiled bride walk slowly up the center aisle toward me. It is my wedding day! Nervous and excited, I lift the veil to see the joyful face of my bride. She has beautiful eyes, smooth rosy cheeks, and blond curls that fall in ringlets around her upturned smiling face. I sense that I love her very much and I am surprised, actually shocked, that I recognize her. I know her in my present life to be CK's mother.

We continue on and I am asked to skip ahead to another important event in my life which relates to my career. I do, and then see myself as a community leader, maybe even a mayor. This reminds me of the lifetime described to me during my first past life reading, in 1989.

In this scene, I get the strong impression that I am working for the town, but from an informal office in my home. My work habits are mediocre, and I try to get by doing as little as possible. I have become a lazy, frustrated man. I'm unhappy and have grown older and heavier. My wife is also frustrated, obese and miserable. We do not do well together; we are not as compatible as we thought we would be. During this era, however, there are no options once we got married. Divorce is not possible. We have stopped making love; we are frustrated and angry at each other and gratify ourselves by taking pleasure in eating lots of food.

One night after getting drunk, I come home seeking the comfort of intimacy with my wife. We've not had sex for a long time. She is unwilling to cooperate, but because of my drunken state, I am unconcerned by her objections. I force myself upon her. As a result of my act of violence, she gets pregnant and our relationship deteriorates even further. I feel terrible for what I did to her. I had acted like a thoughtless animal with no control over my base desires. My feelings of guilt run deep. I am truly not that type of man.

Then I am asked to skip to my proudest moment. I am in a room with my wife, and she is about to give birth to our child.

We are both happy about the baby now. We hope we can work together to raise our child. It will be someone we can both love unconditionally. She gives birth to a boy—I have a son! I am such a proud father. Yet, moments after experiencing this elation, something goes wrong. My wife is hemorrhaging, the bleeding won't stop, and all the mid-wife's efforts are ineffective. My wife is bleeding to death before my eyes and she is cursing me for doing this to her. She dies in my arms.

I go from joy to agony in minutes and blame myself for her death. I believe she would still be alive if I had not forced myself on her and gotten her pregnant. Devastated, I pour the energy of my guilty feelings into the care of my son, whom I recognize as CK in my present life. Since I did not take good care of my wife and feel responsible for her death, it seems logical that I should now take extra good care of our son. I deprived him of his mother and feel the need to make up for it by giving him as much as possible. My guilt blinds me to the fact that I am going overboard, and I take my atonement too far. By giving my son anything and everything his heart desires, he grows up a spoiled, selfish young man. I lost the opportunity I had to help him become a fine human being, one his mother would be proud of. I never say no to him. He grows up defiant, self-centered and inconsiderate, while I get more frustrated and obese. I am caught in a cycle of misery, one of my own making.

As I contemplate the details of this lifetime, I find it fascinating that this memory popped in at this moment while I am trying to come to terms with my breakup with CK. At the end of a relationship, it is normal to have feelings of anger, guilt, and sadness. But I've been having a hard time trying to make sense of what happened. I struggled with figuring out why our relationship failed, why I failed, and why I was drawn to him in the first place. Part of my failure was due to my lack of self-knowledge. I'd never taken the time to get to know myself and what made me happy. My idea about what to expect from a relationship was something quite different from what he envisioned. We had not really talked about expectations or roles.

It feels like I came back in this lifetime, along with CK and his mom, to accomplish some things. As her husband, I did not take care of my wife in the past. I ignored and abused her, and I deprived her of raising her son by indirectly causing her death. In the present, CK's mother got to raise the son she left behind in the past, and have her chance to spoil him. This time, I took good care of her and helped her while her son and I were together. As for my son of the past (CK), in the present I was finally able to set boundaries, say no to him, and make it stick. I stopped spoiling him and stopped giving in to his demands.

Seeing how this past life connects to my present, my current relationships make more sense. There seems to be a karmic balancing occurring.

+++

It is at this point the regression session ends. As I look around the room, I see many of the participants quickly taking notes, writing the details of what they experienced before they forget, like awakening from a dream. I write extensive notes too. I have a lot to think about.

The seminar winds to a close soon after, and though I have enjoyed these last couple of days, it will be good to rest and have time to process all the experiences I have had here. This seminar has been an incredible experience.

***

CONCLUSIONS:

My purpose for signing up for the seminar had been to learn about past lives, but I had come away with much more. I'd learned that there were many ways to meditate, and intuitively tune-in. It excited me to discover that I had been able to sense some things during this seminar. I'd also begun to realize that the insights I'd perceived were valid and not just my imagination. It was getting easier to believe that what I'd seen was not random or coincidental. The growing evidence was getting harder to dismiss. I still had doubts about myself, but when Jack addressed my concern that I was making things up, his pertinent question, "If you were imagining it, why make up such awful events?" had really hit home. Why would I ever want to imagine the traumatic events I had seen and felt?

It surprised me how many tools I could easily use in my daily life. I planned to keep doing guided meditations with the recordings I bought and looked forward to continuing my explorations at home. Being able to perceive my higher self and having a place to meet my spirit guides during meditation would enable me to continue to receive support and guidance from Spirit. I felt reassured that these techniques would help me continue my journey.

The past life experiences I had seen were fantastic and awful. It was incredible to have been able to verify a small part of what that psychic had told me in 1989. During my first past life reading, she had said that I had been a mayor in Germany. I had sensed it was Austria, but the country didn't matter as much as the relationships I'd had there. But the psychic's reading could never compare to my first-hand, experiential recall of my past life memories and the clear knowing of how my lessons connected to my present. Seeing events for myself had been much more helpful.

I had been a little surprised that recalling my past had been somewhat painful, and a little sad that my lives contained only brief moments of joy. I guess I'd been expecting something different. Prior to this seminar, I had spoken to a few people about their past life experiences. They had told me about their fun and interesting lives of purpose and fulfillment. Maybe that's what I had expected. But the infinite details, the agonizing feelings and the terrible traumas were so much deeper than what anyone had described to me.

The intuitive who I had visited in 1989 told me she had seen my current life family and friends while tuning in to my past lives. She had only told me about wonderful, uplifting things from those lifetimes. Her reading had included nothing distasteful. Sometimes people bragged that in their past lives they were someone like Nefertiti or Florence Nightingale. Identifying with famous historical figures seemed to be a common new-age stereotype. Regardless of who they claimed to be, any unpleasant details from their past lives were not included in the narrative. To me, omitting the traumatic details changed the meaning of the entire experience.

Despite the challenges, I had received so much information at this seminar, much more than a simple story. I had discovered the source of some of my feelings, and now I knew why they had come up again in the present. My difficulties in enjoying sex made more sense now. I had always felt I could never really unwind my self-control enough to enjoy the experience. But after seeing this past lifetime, I could see why. I felt responsible for my wife's death. I believed that her pregnancy and subsequent death directly resulted from my loss of self-control when I forced her to have sex with me in my drunken state. Irrationally, I had begun to equate sex with death. My guilt over depriving my son of his mother added to my inner turmoil. However, once I could see these events from my current viewpoint, I had been able to transform my self-recriminations, guilt, and fears.

Knowing what happened in the past also made it easier to understand my actions in the present. I understood why I felt unusually close to CK's mother (my former wife) and always felt the need to support and care for her in the present. It seems that we all play different roles for each other through time. Connecting the past-life memories to the present empowered me to let go of hurts and allow myself to heal.

To have recognized several individuals in the past as people I had had relationships with in my present was shocking to me. Perhaps it was a common thing for souls to be together more than once. But what astounded me most was that I had recognized myself—the similarities in habits, likes, dislikes, and personality quirks. There were many qualities which still expressed themselves in me today. This was a partial validation of what I had been sensing. It proved to me that the person I recognized as me truly was me, no matter what gender, race, ethnicity, sexual preference, age or status I appeared to be. It was my spirit essence clothed in another body.

My life had changed. I felt optimistic that I as I uncovered more past connections, the memories and information could help me learn what I needed to correct in my present. It was my hope that I could release and heal any situation which came up. Past life regression had not been a cure-all, but it was another tool I could use to help myself become a better person.

As I examined my life from this new perspective, I felt better able to accept that there was a logic to what before had seemed to be random situations. My healing had accelerated, because now I understood where some of my concerns had come from and why things had happened the way they did. I could see why I still had such powerful feelings for certain people in my life. With my clearer understanding came release and healing.

I'd learned that it was possible to sense things for myself, and I was beginning to trust that what I was seeing and hearing was not just imagination. Patterns were emerging, so that formerly inexplicable events now seemed to have a clear cause and effect. I had also found tools which would help with my spiritual expansion—meditation and past life regression. The door to my past had definitely opened, and a vast frontier of knowledge and understanding had become available to me.

Questions:

- When I imagine or visualize, am I actually tapping into memories of my subconscious or higher self?

- Is imagination directed? And if so, by whom, my conscious mind, my higher self, or something else, like an angel or spirit guide?

- Does the Higher self remember everything I've ever experienced?

Spiritual Skills Present: Automatic writing, Clairaudience, Claircognizance, Clairempathy, Clairsentience, Clairvoyance, Meditation, Retrocognition

32

Spiritual Retreat – Seeing Clearly

September 9, 1992, 30 yrs.

IT HAD BEEN TWO MONTHS since the past-life seminar where I'd seen a couple of my former lives with my own eyes. I was still trying to make sense of them. It had been difficult learning to accept and release the feelings the memories had brought up.

The second annual Spiritual Retreat was being held soon in the mountains, facilitated by my friends. I was excited to see them and looked forward to this uplifting spiritual boost before I started back to school again. Every conference so far had been a transformative experience, and I hoped that this would be no different...

***

I ARRIVE EARLY AT THE RANCH where the Retreat is being held this year, and while waiting for things to start later in the evening, I chat with a few friends out on the deck. I am catching up with a friend whom I met last year. When he tells me about a movie he's seen recently, including all the gory, violent details, I automatically recoil from such talk, having a very low tolerance for violence and people getting hurt. I react strongly, sharply telling him to stop describing such things to me.

His joking response is, "Wow! Pulling back a bloody stump!"

"Don't say that!" I say, asking him again to not to talk so graphically.

I guess I am still trying to make sense of what I saw at the past life seminar, and I'm a little touchy. I am particularly sensitive to violence relating to the loss of limbs, especially after seeing a past life in which my hands were cut off. As I try to clear the images that have popped into my mind, I hear a quiet voice saying, "You've seen worse than that."

I turn toward the voice and see a retreat participant I haven't met before. It was he who made the comment.

Stunned, I ask, "Why do you say that?"

"You know why," was his enigmatic response.

My thoughts are a jumble. I do know why, but how does he know why I don't want to hear about violence?

I find out later that my new friend has highly developed intuitive abilities; it's incredible. Since I've never met him before, there's no way he could have known that I had recently seen a past life where I'd lost my hands. Has he somehow tapped into my present thoughts and memories, or maybe into my past life? Whatever he did and however he did it, it astonishes me and provides yet another verification of what I saw at the seminar two months ago.

***

CONCLUSIONS:

This experience had been a small but very important step toward realizing that what I had seen for myself about the past was real and not just my imagination. That a stranger I had never met before could know what I had seen at that past life seminar months earlier was amazing. His comments had also proven that there were individuals who could sense things beyond what most people could discern. His observations had also confirmed that what I had seen was accurate. He had picked up the same images as I had, even though there was no way for him to have known. I had not spoken to anyone about it. He could not have known.

It was surprising how events had started to interconnect, and incredible how Spirit was providing me with proof...

Spiritual Skills Present: Claircognizance, Clairsentience, Clairvoyance, Divine timing, Retrocognition

33

A Key to Violence...

September 19, 1992, 30 yrs.

BY THIS POINT IN MY LIFE, I'd become aware that I had an extreme sensitivity to violence. I'd found I could not tolerate witnessing people being hurt on television shows, in movies, or in any other situation. It had become unbearable. Whatever the injuries or traumas I'd seen, real or fake, I felt within me. The pain others felt, I felt. The trauma, sadness, fear they felt, I felt. The more graphic the violence, the more abhorrent my experience became. I had to stop watching movies rated PG-13 or higher after going to a show which had been advertised as an uplifting family movie. It might have been inspiring if it hadn't had explicit scenes of bare-handed fist-fights which had shown the combatants getting bloodied on the big screen. Each time someone's face was struck and blood sprayed across the screen, I had sunk lower in my seat. That movie had just about done me in.

I had tried many times in my life to toughen up; especially at movie theaters, where I would remind myself that they were only actors in makeup. Yet at that PG-13 family movie, watching 30-foot tall close-ups of gushing blood and smashed faces, I could not halt my natural feelings of empathy, even after I had repeatedly told myself, "It's just a movie, it's just a movie." Trying not to feel hadn't worked. I had been horrified by what was happening to the characters on the screen, and with each blow, it had gotten worse. I felt physically ill, nauseated and light-headed, but because I had gone to the movies with a group of people, I felt obligated to stay. So I had closed my eyes, covered my ears, and desperately hoped that the fight scene would end soon.

My friends and family had not understood my problem. For me, to be sensitive to violence in a culture where violence is often idealized was strange to them. It never made sense to me either. It was just as difficult for me to understand them. How could they think that repeated acts of violence, death, and destruction were entertaining? Some of my friends enjoyed the realistic close-ups of the graphic scenes. They marveled at the filming and the technology. They hadn't had an uprush of any feelings, except that they thought it was cool. But witnessing that much reality in high definition, and hearing it in surround sound, made each act of violence more traumatic for me to watch; to experience.

After the trauma I felt during that last PG-13 movie, I gave up trying to make myself less sensitive and instead became more careful of what images I allowed myself to see. I had finally realized that whatever I saw stayed in my mind. It seemed I had a photographic memory that replayed images and sounds over and over, whether the visions had been pleasant or not. So it wasn't necessarily the first exposure that had been bad, it was the endless repeats that were the worst. I had accepted that I was a sensitive person, though I was still very curious why. I also wondered what lessons connected to my condition.

I had read that qualities or behaviors people couldn't stand in others were actually indicators of things they didn't like in themselves. If that was true, then I really needed an answer!

Was there some kind of violence within me which I'd been unable to accept? Was that what made me so sensitive to violence when I saw others doing it? I'd hoped to find an explanation soon. I had asked Spirit about the source of my sensitivity several times over the years, most recently at the September Retreat and the July seminar. I hoped to receive answers, eventually.

But now, it was time for me to get focused on my current challenges. I had returned to college to finish my bachelor's degree and was in the midst of my first semester at a four-year school. I had a full load of classes, which included physics and anatomy. Busy was an understatement. I was studying every spare moment, especially when my toddler was asleep.

This evening, while studying for an exam, my spirit guide dropped in unexpectedly...

***

WHILE MAKING FLASH CARDS for the chapter I'm studying, I sense that my guide, Achaeus, has come in and is telling me it is time for a break. He has something to show me. Reluctantly, I put my book down and start meditating. I soon find myself walking down the tunnel leading to the past as I had done before. Even before stepping out of the dark tunnel, I see a medicine man from an ancient South American civilization, Aztec or Maya. I don't know why I think he is a medicine man; I just know that he is. Images flash in too: a human's skull being smashed, a beating heart ripped from a live victim's chest. What am I seeing? This is not very pleasant.

Continuing, I emerge from the tunnel into the past and discover I *am* the medicine man. There are bone bracelets strung around my wrists and calves, and leather sandals on my feet. I'm wearing a skirt of leather with feathers, topped off by a black-feathered headdress. The upper half of my face is painted black, and my skin is brown. I ask my guide why I have been mostly men in my past-life incarnations so far. Achaeus answers,

> There are slight variations of experience associated with each gender, but to have insight into childbirth, you must choose to be female. Some differences are physical, but most are social, relating to opportunities to experience power, freedom and love. To achieve balance, we must spend some time being each.

I had not thought about past lives this way.

As I move further into this lifetime, I discover I am Aztec and that as a young man, I was a talented and compassionate healer. As my skills grew, I became well known and got appointed to a prominent position by the leaders of my society. It was the equivalent of a Royal appointment, a tremendous change in my social standing. As time passes, I see myself consumed and corrupted by the power at my command.

I feel myself change from being a gentle, loving healer into a brutal, sadistic tormentor. I use my position and power to conduct experiments on people, intentionally inflicting wounds and breaking bones, supposedly so I can learn how to treat and heal these types of injuries. But I don't stop there. I feel no remorse or empathy for the pain and suffering I inflict on my subjects.

My values and self-respect are so compromised that I have become a hollow shell of a person. Whatever spark of inner decency I may have had is gone, forcibly snuffed out. My emotions are so blocked off, I feel nothing at all. Being so empty inside, my life becomes a sadistic series of meaningless events. I perform human sacrifices. I pull the beating hearts from the bodies of victims amid cheering crowds and cause excruciating pain in people who are sent to me to persuade and punish. As time passes, I grow more depraved; the greater the pain I'm able to induce in my subjects, the greater is my sadistic pleasure.

Women are a favorite target to abuse, torture, and use in cruel experimentation. The added dimension of being able to use women for unwilling sex provides me with many opportunities to exert my power and domination. I often try to see how much I can do to a woman's body before she dies from her wounds. If a female survives my attentions and gets pregnant, she is thought of as being exceptionally strong and gains respect from the community and more freedom. It is a twisted life centered around my obsession with power, greed, lust, and anything else I can think of to stimulate any sort of true feeling within me. I am empty inside, devoid of emotion and never satisfied, even after my experiments conclude or my victims die. The pleasure I feel at their suffering is superficial and fleeting. The emptiness continues, like a dark, gaping maw of bitterness and despair.

My guide brings me out of this experience just before there is a noisy outside distraction in my present life surroundings. It would have been disconcerting to be unexpectedly yanked out of a deep trance. Many times during deep meditations, I feel a nudge to come out of it in perfect timing so I won't be shocked when something interrupts, like a knock on the door, a phone call, or an unexpected noise. The timing is quite amazing, and it is yet another way for me to know there is a higher power with a broader perspective looking out for and helping me.

Out of the past and talking with my guide now, he tells me that my current sensitivity connects to this Aztec lifetime. In my present, I am horrified by abuse, psychological terror, graphic violence and pain. In my past, I felt nothing, no empathy, no sympathy, remorse or mercy for those who were hurt by my acts of violence. He adds,

> Things that you have strong feelings of dislike towards now tend to be things you have done in the past at one time or another. People and events in your life provide clues and act as mirrors, showing you what you need to look at and resolve within yourself. The unbalanced energy of your thoughts and feelings draws people and situations into your life, providing you with opportunities to discover and balance unlearned lessons.

This explanation makes my strong dislike of violence seem more logical to me. I was the one committing violent acts before without feeling, and now I am traumatized by feeling it when I witness similar events. It is like an equal and opposite reaction, an emotional and energetic consequence for my lack of compassion and empathy towards others in the past. What I have sown, I am now reaping.

CONCLUSIONS:

As I looked at this lifetime from a broader perspective, I could see now why I have been so motivated to help people heal their hearts, and why I couldn't tolerate violence. Perhaps I found it unacceptable to do harm or watch harmful things being done to others because, on some level, it reminded me of what I had done in the past. I'd felt nothing then, but felt everything now. It didn't feel good. I understood myself better now, but I still felt bad for what I had done and I was deeply ashamed of what I became in that life.

I also took away from this past lifetime a better understanding of why I had hesitated to step into a leadership role in my present. Since I had been such a brutal leader in my past, I could comprehend why I was reluctant to put myself into a similar situation in the present. There was a strong possibility that I could be corrupted by the influence of power, and I could experience a return of my negative behaviors. In that past life, I'd also felt I was better than others. The feelings and lives of other people were unimportant and worth little to me. Now I held strong convictions that we are all equal, regardless of birthplace, gender, fame, orientation, wealth or social position. My view is that each person has an equally important role in the universe, including our animal friends and the various forms of life on planet Earth.

Although I was grateful that I received an answer from Spirit, the timing made it a challenge to focus on my schoolwork. I hoped this kind of spontaneous past life regression would not happen often.

Spiritual Skills Present: Clairaudience, Claircognizance, Clairempathy, Clairsentience, Clairvoyance, Divine timing

34

Spiritual Retreat in the Trees

June 9, 1996, 33 yrs.

MY SPIRITUAL PROGRESS HAD SLOWED down for a few years when the responsibilities I had taken on threatened to overwhelm me. I was going to college, single parenting, working, and caring for my terminally ill mother, which meant my days and nights were full. The only respite I had allowed myself was the rare occasional Retreat or Conference. Events like these inspired my heart and soul and kept me moving forward on the path.

But as my mother required more care, and my homework and workload increased, so did my need for spiritual support. I found it by occasionally attending the meetings of a local metaphysical group. I had first met these people at a spiritual bookshop in 1992, where they'd picked me from the audience to take part in a demonstration of their past life regression techniques. It delighted me to discover that Johnathan, a friend from the 1988 Metaphysical Conference, was also a member of this local group. When I walked into their space to attend one of their regular meetings and saw him, I knew I had found a spiritual lifeline!

Estate duties had kept me busy and numb after my mother passed away. But once her business affairs were complete, my feelings of grief and sadness had risen to the surface. I needed more support.

I had begun to attend the spiritual group's meetings more frequently, so when the opportunity had arisen to go on a weekend retreat with them, I had tentatively decided to go. I had been scared to join them, since the destination was far from home and I still didn't know the people very well. But I went anyway. I'd really needed a change of scene; a break from what I had been dealing with. Johnathan also planned to attend, which helped me feel much more at ease. Thankfully, I'd been able to hitch a ride to the Retreat with him or I probably wouldn't have gone. I'd been feeling the urge to resume my spiritual journey, and this was an excellent opportunity to move in that direction...

***

THE WEEKEND GATHERING is being held at a lovely retreat center not too far from the ocean. We are staying in a large converted home that has several rooms for sleeping, similar to a bed-and-breakfast. My favorite part of the place is a beautiful meeting hall that is built almost entirely out of glass and surrounded by redwood trees. At night, when I look up, I can see the stars and moon, and in the morning, sunbeams peek through the trees. It is an amazing place that feels very peaceful and nurturing, exactly what I need right now.

The first evening, one of the first activities we do is a drumming circle, which is so fun that we end up doing it every night. We place sacred objects, candles, and instruments of all sorts in the center of the large circle of attendees. People have brought drums, rattles, bells and many other unusual instruments, which we share and play when we feel inspired to do so. We drum inside the glass hall, where the beauty of the stars and moon shining through the glass adds to the total effect.

It begins with one person who starts beating a drum, then another person adds in and then another until we all are playing together. Each person is playing whatever rhythm they intuitively sense they should, which seems like we would end up with a crazy bunch of noise, but we don't. The rhythms somehow become synchronous, work harmoniously together, and everything seems to fit. No one signals when to stop playing, but somehow we do. One by one, people drop out and then suddenly, with perfect timing, the rest of us stop playing and it ends.

I had experienced this synchronous stopping and starting before, when I had been out in nature. Without warning, the air would fill with the sound of hundreds of frogs or cicadas that would start croaking or chirping simultaneously, surrounding me with song; then, just as abruptly, they would stop—all at once. After a brief period of eerie quiet, they would start up again, all together, in unison. Spooky. I don't know how this is possible. Is it energy, vibration, intuition, or some other invisible connection? Perhaps these experiences are a way of showing me that music and songs connect people and animals in ways I am not yet fully aware of. I am thrilled to take part in this drumming. It is such an amazing experience!

Next we do a meditation, and to my surprise, I pop into another spontaneous past life experience.

+++

I SEE MYSELF AS a happy young blonde girl running carefully through a meadow. I am carrying a pail of milk home from my grandma's house; she lives near us, just across the woods from me and my family. I hear myself thinking, "I have to get this milk home to mama for the baby."

A sense of dread comes over me as I watch myself hurry down the path that winds its way through the woods. Not long after I get to the thicket, two men attack me, throwing me to the ground, spilling the milk. I am crying, caring more about the milk than the men, not realizing I should be concerned about other things at that moment. One man grabs my arms and holds me down, while the other is ripping my dress and bonnet. He immobilizes my legs, then rapes me. I am screaming and wishing I were bigger, big enough to fight them off.

Out of nowhere, an enormous bear looms up behind them and attacks the two men, killing them and ripping them into pieces. But I don't stay to watch the men die. As soon as the bear pulls the men off of me, I'm up and running for my life, my clothes still askew and tripping me. I run away as fast as I can, not bothering to look back. I run until my legs are shaking and my lungs feel like they are about to burst. I trip and sprawl headlong onto the soft forest floor near a tree. I can feel the dirt beneath my face and hands. Grasping at its softness, I feel it working its way between my fingers. Still crying, I pause and breathe in the earth's smell, and somehow I sense support and take comfort from the ground and the trees. With a burst of anger I shout to the ground, "If I was big I could have got away!"

+++

The images black out after that, and I am back in the present with the meditation ending. What a crazy welcome on the first night of the Retreat! I did not expect this. I am relieved when another drumming round begins. After seeing these new past life traumas, the rhythms of the drums put me at ease.

The next night, during meditation, my guides pop in, as well as a familiar ascended Master, Jesus. His presence is very reassuring, and it lessens the trauma of the scenes I witnessed last night.

After the drumming, the owner of the retreat center, David and our chef, Jenny, introduce themselves to our group. They are both kind and seem a little familiar to me.

I am inspired by David's sacred approach to things. I feel a sense of connection with him. The way he speaks of his retreat center with such reverence and how he presents himself, it feels as though we are kindred spirits. He seems so connected to nature and the earth, like I feel at times. But there is also something familiar about him; his voice, the way he looks, something in his eyes. There are many objects on display in his place which relate to dolphins, hawks and owls. There are feathers, crystals, driftwood and photographs which remind me of my own connections to these lovely creatures, and the experiences I have had with them.

The next day, the group is going on an outing to the beach to see the tide pools and enjoy the ocean. I'm waiting in Johnathan's van for people to finish getting into the cars for our excursion. When look up, I see David on the deck with his coffee, watching. I feel as if he is watching me, but that seems unlikely. I wave in case he is watching, and he waves back solemnly. When I see him watching, and then waving back, I get an overwhelming sense that he was a Native American chief in a past life. I rarely get such powerful impressions about people, but this comes to mind so clearly, along with the sense that he was a father protector, and that we knew each other in the past.

I have similar experiences with Jenny, the chef. One afternoon, I walk through the kitchen and see her with a bowl of batter in her hands. She is looking around the kitchen. It's clear she is in distress. I ask her what's wrong, and she says that something is missing in the brownies. She offers me a taste and asks,

"Does it need more chocolate?"

We work on it together, laughing as we fix the batter and have fun as we spend some time relaxing in the kitchen. Impulsively, I tell her I feel like I have known her a long time and how much I am enjoying her company. She says she has been having the same feelings.

On the last night of the Retreat, our host David, his mate Linda, and Jenny join our group meditation and drumming circle. Their presence makes it even more special. When the drumming circle winds to a close, the clairvoyant, who is part of the spiritual group, shares some of his insights. He tells us that many Native American spirits have been around us this weekend. He has sensed their presence, especially during the drumming circles and near the trees that thrive around the retreat center.

When it comes time to return home, we gather for a group hug and photos. Jenny and David have come out to say goodbye and David ends up taking the pictures with everyone's cameras. I hug Jenny and a few others, and we disperse to get our things packed up. Before I go, I work up the courage to ask David for permission to take a picture of him and the retreat center. He agrees. I quickly take the photo and then we share a hug.

I get my things loaded up and wait for the others. I see David and we hug again, this time kissing each other on the cheek. We talk more while we wait. He tells me he may come to join our group occasionally, and that he hopes I will come back. Uncharacteristically for me, I encourage him to call me if he is coming to town, and I give him my phone number. I tell him I have a feeling that I've known him before and am delighted to find out he is feeling the same way. He tells me about some places he has lived to see if we have ever lived near each other before or if our paths have crossed previously. Yet another case of déjà vu.

We don't discover a time when we have been together in this life, but it is always exhilarating to meet someone I think I know, and then find out they recognize me too. It is very validating, even if we can't figure out the specifics of how we know each other; it is enough to know that we both recognize each other and that there is a connection.

These déjà vu encounters usually give rise to a flood of mixed emotions. There is joy in meeting again, plus sadness and frustration at not being able to discover the common thread that connects us. I have shared mutual feelings of déjà vu with several people now: someone at the first metaphysical conference, a co-worker, a distant family member I'd never met before, and now with Jenny and David. Recognizing these special people is both comforting and exciting.

Although I've noticed a pattern emerging relating to what happens after we meet again. When we find each other, there is a rush of delight and hope, and I assume we will maintain our newly discovered connection. But thus far, it hasn't worked out that way. Invariably, we are drawn apart, and don't establish close relationships in the present because of various circumstances. I haven't yet found out where or when these connections originated, but I hope that someday I will understand. I'm so grateful for having met them! It has added a sprinkling of magic to my life. It has happened so many times now that I think there has to be a purpose, and an uplifting, perfect timing aspect to it.

This Retreat marks the beginning of a new association with this spiritual group and friendships that I hope will last for many years to come.

***

CONCLUSIONS:

I had gone to this Retreat to find answers to questions about things that had been puzzling me in my present. The experiences that occurred there partially solved some of the mysteries. The past life that I'd popped into partly explained some of my current life attitudes.

In the present, I had never really cared if milk got spilled, quite unlike other members of my family. Running had never been a favorite either, though that was partly because I had asthma as a child and it was hard for me. But even when I was feeling well, running had never been appealing. The past life horrors and traumas which I had recalled might have added to my dislike of violence and gory things. In one life, I had abused and hurt others as an Aztec doctor, but in this past, I had also experienced the opposite: I had been a victim of violence.

On the more pleasant side of things, I had often felt invigorated by the smell and feel of fresh earth, particularly the soft blanket of leaves and pine needles that cover the forest floor. While spending time in nature, many times I had felt comforted and supported by the green growing plants and the trees. These attitudes all seemed like they could connect to the past life I had just witnessed.

But what struck me most was that when I had been attacked in the past, I had wished that I could be bigger and stronger so I could've gotten away or fought my attackers well enough to escape the pain, injury, and humiliation. In my present life, whenever I had felt threatened or unsafe, my body tended to get heavier and stronger. But now I felt that my body had become too big. Were there other lifetimes where I had felt unprotected? Could those lives also connect to my present-life body size? What did I need to do now so that the past could no longer impact my present well-being? How could I remain strong, healthy, and safe, and yet be a more comfortable size? I hoped I would gain more insights and find solutions to my weight situation soon.

My new experiences with Jesus (or Master J, as they affectionately called him) were gratefully welcome. His comforting presence and energy provided such a calming influence. Their use of the term Ascended Master had me curious as to what that meant. Since one or more Ascended Masters had popped in during the drumming session that first night, I wanted to know more about them.

The retreat facilitator told me that Master was a title of deep honor and respect. Masters are advanced beings of light that have overcome space and time, and have evolved beyond the need for a physical body. They have achieved high levels of spiritual development. Many of them had areas of specialization, similar to medical doctors who specialize in certain aspects of the physical body. They could be called upon to provide help and guidance. An Ascended Master had attained balance and control of their thoughts, emotions, and the energies connected to their past. These beings could also consciously control their use of the etheric energy of God or prana.

After this brief introduction, I looked forward to learning more about the Ascended Masters.

Since I had experienced another spontaneous past life during the Retreat, I decided it was time to seek professional help. I wanted to explore the past in a more conscious way, rather than waiting for past-lives to pop in without warning. Though I had received some answers, so many more questions had arisen and I felt I needed help.

Questions:

- Why do we meet people we seem to know?

- Is there a way to understand where we know them from?

- Would knowing the origins of these connections interfere with my current lesson opportunities?

- If nothing was an accident, then why did these déjà vu experiences happen? What purpose did they serve?

- Were déjà vu encounters meant to provide me with the motivation to continue on my path of spiritual self-discovery?

Spiritual Skills Present: Clairalience, Clairaudience, Claircognizance, Clairempathy, Clairsentience, Clairvoyance, Divine timing, Intuition, Retrocognition, Synchronicity

Section Three, Part One – Tentative Proof

Delving deeper, going into my past,

I am looking for healing and

Peace at long last.

I am starting to sense more,

Learning to believe and Trust in what I see.

The things I am seeing are starting to explain

Some of the mysterious events

That my present life contains.

35

Past-Life Regression Therapy Begins

June 3, 1997, 34 yrs.

I HAD BECOME better friends with people in the local spiritual group after I attended their retreat in 1996. I'd started going to their meetings and classes regularly and discovered that the group leaders conducted past-life regression sessions. That had intrigued me. Perhaps they could help me with the past life memories that had been popping in. Maybe they could improve my understanding of them and facilitate the release of the traumas that came with them.

Several times during my spiritual journey, I had heard that physical disease in the present life is likely caused by unresolved emotional issues from the past. If true, then my weight issues could have roots in my childhood and/or past lives. Perhaps if I tried to resolve my issues on a spiritual level, maybe I could finally achieve a lasting improvement in my health and fitness on the physical level. Until now, I had tried every other way to lose weight without lasting success.

I felt I needed help in order to explore my past effectively. My earlier experiences with past life memories had felt traumatic and overwhelming. When these memories popped in spontaneously, I didn't know how to deal with the uprush of feelings that came with them. I would be distracted for days, weeks, or months, which made it challenging to maintain my focus on current life goals. I was so grateful for the gifts of these memories, because along with the traumas came answers, growth, and expanded awareness. But if the events of the past connected to my present, then I wanted to be able to retrieve these memories consciously, rather than having to deal with them popping in at inopportune times. I wanted to gain a greater understanding of myself and receive noticeable healing.

Calling in experts seemed like it would be the best way to get clear, measurable results. I had nothing to lose, so I made an appointment, specifically asking for help with weight loss. I was told I could get results in six sessions, which sounded great to me. At last, I began to hope that I could be healthy and fit again.

My journey through my past lives had begun in earnest...

Pastor's Daughter

I AM WORKING WITH two people, a facilitator and a clairvoyant. The facilitator guides me into a meditative state while the clairvoyant tunes in and is able to see past life events that are relevant to the situation I have asked for help with. As the clairvoyant describes each scene, I am able to visualize what he describes, and soon I am caught up in the memories and feelings that arise.

This lifetime takes place during the early colonial period in the United States. I am the attractive, eligible daughter of our small town's highly esteemed pastor. He is well respected by the people of the town. My mother is not present. It is not clear to me if she died or what happened, but death seems most likely.

With no mother around, I am the woman taking care of running the household. There is a lot of work, but I am young, strong and capable of hard labor. As the daughter of a Christian holy man, I have been raised believing in God. I feel Jesus is a part of my life, and that Spirit is always near me and hears my prayers.

But my life changes when my father comes home one evening drunk and angry. Incomprehensible and blinded by liquor, he destroys objects in our home until I become the target for his fury. He comes after me, beats and viciously rapes me, then passes out. Devastated, I feel betrayed by my earthly father who is supposed to love and protect me, and betrayed by God, the father, and Jesus, my spiritual protectors. How can they let this happen to me, a devoted, faithful believer? I feel filthy and bruised physically, emotionally, mentally, and spiritually numb. I soak in a small tub bath, curled up in a ball trying to wash away what just happened. But no amount of soap and water can cleanse my mind of the memory of that event. I pray, begging for help from God.

I pray it won't happen again, and that this will be an isolated incident, but it is not. The abuse continues, brutal and savage. I try to seek help from others. Frightened and ashamed, I try to hint to other townspeople that my father is not the nice guy he seems to be. When he finds out that I have been raising suspicion about his reputation, he beats me severely in order to silence me.

I continue to pray, hoping for some kind of spiritual support to deliver me from this situation, but no help arrives. Suffering his monstrosities in silence, whilst listening to others praise his good moral character, infuriates me. The bottled up anger and frustration of being brutally abused builds into a savage internal fury. Feeling abandoned by friends, family and unsupported by God; the next time he attacks, something in me snaps. I fight like a wild animal. I manage to put my hands on a knife and irrationally think that if I cut off his penis, then he can no longer violate me with it. I accomplish this and shove the offending body part into his mouth, letting him choke on it, just as his cruel abuse has been choking the life and spirit out of me.

As I stand over his dying body, trying to catch my breath from the efforts of our struggle, some of my sanity returns. Horrified, I begin to realize the full measure of what I have just done. I panic and run away, but with each step, a swirl of conflicting emotions starts cascading through me. I think about the tremendous sin of this act and I am fearful of the consequences, both from the physical and the spiritual realms.

I am also ashamed to admit that part of me feels immense relief and satisfaction at his demise. I believe my actions were justified as an act of self-defense and, in a way, a fair consequence for his actions. As the victim, I feel like he got a partial payback of what he was dealing out to me. Since I feel angry that God has abandoned me and has ignored my prayers, I do not feel bad about abandoning the moral directives of His commandments.

I try to evade capture, fearful of what will happen, but it is of no use. I am easily tracked down and caught. At the trial I am given, I lose all hope that I will receive fair and just treatment, since my judge and jury are the devoted followers of the beloved pastor. The way he dies, and that his own ungrateful daughter did it, seals my fate. I am convicted and scheduled to be publicly executed.

My execution is unimaginable and as heinous as my crime. I am stripped of clothing, hair cut off, eyes gouged out, I am tied to a wooden post, put in the back of a wagon and paraded through town where villagers throw stones and cut me with their knives. The pain and humiliation are beyond comprehension. I cannot believe how much damage and pain a human body can endure and still be alive. To finish the job, they burn me at the stake, which sends my pain level soaring, and finally, life slips away. As my spirit steps out of that body, the first thing I see is Jesus waiting for me.

"Where were you!?" I lash out, my sense of betrayal and frustration still strong. He replies,

> I have been with you all along, but your anger and hatred have made it difficult for you to sense my presence. Your reaction to the situation has filled you with so much negativity that you could not, would not receive the help that had been sent in answer to your prayers.

As he speaks, the power of his presence permeates the waves of anger, and the other swirling emotions I am still caught up in. Potent energy of pure peacefulness radiates from him. As I allow it, my chaotic pain starts to dissolve, and I feel calmed by his gentle, loving presence. Despite all that has happened, what was hurting me most was the thought that I had been abandoned by the Spiritual being that I so deeply believed in, and held so dear. Now I understood that he had NOT abandoned me. I knew now that I might fail the trials and lessons that had been wrought for me, and I might not comprehend the purpose of them, but I would always be supported by Spirit, regardless of the outcome.

***

CONCLUSIONS:

Opening up this past life was a crazy, intense, remarkable, awful experience. The depth of emotions which had come up was difficult to convey. I had never felt such rage, despair, disgust and hopelessness as I had during the time I'd spent reliving this past life. The facilitator had helped me release and heal some of the turbulent emotions which came along with the memories. But an hour session wasn't long enough to deal with so many layers of residual feelings and so many traumas. The facilitator told me to continue the releasing process at home by remembering each scene, noticing what emotions came up, and asking Spirit to help clear them. This process helped immensely. Journaling and meditation brought even more insights and clarity.

My struggle, coming to terms with the events I saw in this past life, resulted in helping me get a clear understanding about several issues. Having been a victim rather than an instigator as I was in the Aztec lifetime, I realized that violence could cause internal trauma in a victim on many levels beyond the physical. I had felt so demoralized and powerless from being hurt by someone I should've been able to trust. I thought my father loved me and would therefore protect me from harm, not be the one inflicting it. When I'd been an Aztec doctor, I had been oblivious to the many layers of hurt and pain which I dealt out to my victims. I hadn't been able to feel it, and so never understood the nuances of why what I was doing was wrong.

My thoughts and feelings were a mass of confusion trying to reconcile what should have happened as a pastor's daughter versus what had actually happened. My self-esteem in that life had plummeted with the thought that if I was not worthy of my own father's respect and protection, then I wasn't worth anything to anyone. By being treated like garbage, I had felt disposable.

It had also occurred to me that since others considered me physically attractive, maybe I had somehow brought this on myself or had asked for it, and deserved the treatment I had received. These thoughts only increased my feelings of self-loathing and self-disgust.

Stepping back from these feelings of the past, I could see that if I compared the Aztec lifetime and this one, there might be some kind of payback or karma happening. After all, I had hurt and tortured so many as an Aztec doctor. Maybe this was a part of God's justice. I got back what I gave out.

But it had not felt like the lessons were only about justice, or an eye for an eye. Part of my lessons must have related to holding fast to my beliefs and having faith, despite the extremely challenging circumstances. I had followed the path of hate and anger. Had I remained faithful, things might have turned out differently, even though I saw no other options at the time. If I'd trusted that Spirit would be there when I'd asked for support, I might have made better choices. The presence of Master J (Jesus) after my death proved to me that he was there when I'd called to him, and that my prayers had been heard.

Not long after this session, I discovered a painting that was a perfect reminder of the lesson from that lifetime: I would always have the love and support of Spirit. The principal subject was a wonderful likeness of the Ascended Master, Jesus, looking very much as I had seen him in my session. Seated on his lap sat a lovely child, happy and trusting. The child may have been painted to look like any number of children, but I strongly felt that it looked like me. The child's face perfectly illustrated that she felt supported and cared for in his loving embrace. This painting emanated the love, comfort and support that he gave me in that lifetime and beyond, and served as an excellent reminder of his presence. Regardless of whether I could sense him, I knew now that Spirit was and would always be nearby.

I purchased the painting and hung it by my bedside. It was the first thing I saw in the morning, and the last thing I saw at night. It hangs there to this day, reminding me that I will always receive unconditional love and support, and that there is a dependable presence of loving beings nearby ready to help, no matter how things seem to be going.

The experiences of this session felt connected to my present weight issues. Maybe I subconsciously wished to be overweight and unattractive in the present in order to discourage others from being sexually drawn to me. The violent abuse from a trusted man in my past seemed a logical reason for feeling uneasy with potential sexual partners in my present. My current low self-esteem could also be an echo of my dismal feelings of self-worth from that prior life. But now that I had confronted and released the traumas of the past, I hoped I would see an improvement in my confidence and health. My intimate relationships might even improve thanks to my new insights.

Similar to the Aztec life, this lifetime contained traumas which might also contribute to my abhorrence of violence. However, the greatest gift I got from this experience was meeting and sensing Master J. Remembering this firsthand experience would remind me that—no matter what—I am not alone, and that I am loved.

Spiritual Skills Present: Claircognizance, Clairempathy, Clairsentience, Clairvoyance, Divine timing, Energy Healing, Retrocognition

36

Bishop or Something Else?

June 10, 1997, 34 yrs.

EVEN THOUGH IT HAD been traumatic, my first session was such an incredible experience that I was soon ready for another journey into my past. It surprised me that the first session had helped me to release hurts and accept my current life experiences as much as it had. By signing up for another session, I hoped to continue to delve into the lessons of my past and find connections to my present life traumas...

IN THIS LIFE I AM an attractive young woman of marriageable age many centuries ago. My parents are influential people in a position of authority. We live in an enormous castle or château in the country. One unusual feature of this place is that there is a large windowless room, a chapel where my parents often spend time. They usually send me to my room when they go in there. This seems strange to me; I don't feel like my parents are that religious.

There is also a man from the church, a bishop who often goes with them into the Chapel. I am curious and suspicious about these chapel meetings. When my parents come out of there, they seem distracted, as if they are in some kind of trance or under the influence of something when they emerge. They don't seem drunk, but it is as if they are somehow being controlled.

One evening when I am ordered away, I pretend to leave, and then duck behind a large object in the back of the chapel. It is such an odd room, no seating, no benches or pews; but there are several stone slabs that stand vertically at intervals throughout the long rectangular room. The darkness feels sinister to me. Don't most chapels have stained-glass windows? The only light in the darkness comes from crudely fashioned chandeliers made of black metal, hanging from the ceiling by chains. I stand motionless behind a slab near the back doors. I am apprehensive, but I must discover what's going on in here.

This turns out not to be such a good idea. I see them doing strange rituals, where they are drinking blood and eating—I'm not sure what. The bishop doesn't seem so holy to me now. Unfortunately, I am discovered and escorted from the room. My parents are seriously displeased with me. The bishop is taking me back to my chambers. I walk in ahead of him and turn to find he has followed me into my room. I don't understand and ask him to leave. He does not.

Something is happening. I am afraid of him, but I feel something else too. I am experiencing a sudden, very strong physical attraction to the bishop. He is much older than I, middle-aged, decades older than what I have wished for in a mate, so I don't understand why I am having this strong and sudden uprush of feelings. I have never felt attracted to him before, but now I feel like a moth drawn to a flame. It feels very crazy and shameful, yet exciting too.

He approaches me, which scares me, yet I am also becoming more and more aroused. He grabs me by the arms and says,

"You will obey my every command," then he stares at me with a dark penetrating gaze.

He starts kissing and touching me. I am frightened, but part of me also feels overwhelming excitement. He quickly gets me on the bed and is having his way with me physically. A man has never done this to me before. I've never felt so alive! I am anxious and in pain, yet I feel such pleasure. It is intoxicating.

I feel strange. It is like my mind has stepped back and is cowering in the corner while my body revels and throbs with pleasure. To my rational mind, it is rape; but my body, acting on its own, is so cooperative that it seems like it doesn't belong to me. My mind watches, unable to influence my body's actions. The bishop finishes and starts walking away, leaving me sprawled on the bed.

I watch him and halfway to the door, he changes. His human persona shifts into a dark cloud of moving energy. Stunned, I stare as the entity moves toward me again. It is another sexual attack, but nothing like it was before. Sensation after sensation simultaneously all over my body, waves of pleasure and excitement, all of my erogenous zones perfectly stimulated, all at once. I am writhing, moaning; the sensations are intense and still growing. Then suddenly, it all stops, just before the sensations peak. Shocked, I cry out, begging him to continue. I want to keep feeling this ecstasy. The abrupt stop from such intense pleasure is supremely painful.

Without warning, the bishop reappears in his physical body, standing next to my bed. I throw myself to the ground at his feet, arms wrapped around his knees, hysterically pleading for more, tears streaming down my face. He waits. After a few minutes, my mind re-engages with my body. I calm down and stand, looking up into his face. There is no emotion apparent.

His eyes are dark, unreadable. Such a lack of presence, such darkness, seems evil to me.

He says, "You will cooperate fully with everything you're told to do."

Without a backward glance, he walks out of my room, closing the door behind him. I am alone. Alone and desolate.

What just happened? I don't understand. I am so ashamed at my response, my lack of self-control, and my inability to resist his unwanted and improper advances. My life is ruined. I am no longer a maiden, unfit for a legitimate marriage. I'm doomed.

When the bishop next returns to the château, my shame deepens as I realize that part of me is excited, and wants to experience more pleasure. But when I think about the encounter with him in my room, how I lost control of my body, and remember the pleasure bordering on pain, I truly don't want to experience it again.

I try to warn my parents that this so-called bishop is not what he seems and can't be trusted, but they don't listen and will hear no talk against him. They are completely taken in by him and tell me they have made arrangements for me to marry him. I am horrified at this news and I try to explain what he did to me, how he changed and what he really is, a dark being, a cloud of evil. They don't believe me.

Unbeknownst to us all, the bishop has quietly slipped into the back of the room as I am describing him to my parents. Shortly after that, my parents go off in their dazed manner, and I am escorted to my room. The bishop soon joins me in my chamber and threatens to kill my parents if I ever try to betray him again. He shape shifts, and tortures me as he did before, repeatedly bringing me to heights of ecstasy, but never quite to fulfillment. My agony and frustration grows as does my despair.

As the days and weeks go by, his tortuous visits continue, and I become more nervous and distraught. I cannot see an end to this situation, nor the possibility of freedom from this unholy alliance. One afternoon, after making sure the bishop is not expected, I plead again with my parents to free me from this arrangement. They don't listen to me and end up confining me to my quarters.

Now a prisoner in my rooms, high in a tower, I fear there will be no escape. I dread the bishop's return, yet like an addict, I crave his company. My wild, contradictory feelings only increase my self-loathing, depression and despair. I am alone and no one believes me.

The servants would listen and might even believe me if I tell them everything. But how can I explain? My situation is so embarrassing. They might see it as sacrilegious, plus it is so ridiculously far-fetched. Who would believe such inconceivable nonsense? Even if they were willing to help me, they would probably be powerless to stop him. With no one to talk to, desperate and alone, I turn to God and wonder if He will believe and help me. Can miracles really happen? I pray for one.

I am shaking from want of release. I am in agony waiting for the bishop's return; wanting to be with him, but apprehensive both of him and my response to him. Time passes slowly, and my hopelessness grows.

I know I cannot continue to endure this bizarre, sinful existence. I hate this, yet must admit with self-disgust that I am addicted to the stimulation, always hoping to reach the peak but never do. It is a torture that is indescribable in its intensity and scope. I had hoped to have feelings of warmth, love and connection with my future mate. But those qualities are absent from whatever this is. All I experience are the purely physical sensations taken to the extreme beyond pleasure to pain. Having no choice in the matter makes it worse; adding to the looming threat that my parents will die should I refuse. I cannot go on. I cannot allow this creature to continue to torture and abuse me like this. I must stop this somehow. I see no way out except one—to end my own life.

I don't want to die. I am only 18 years old with my entire life ahead of me. But I cannot live under these conditions, day after day, month after month, year after year, without any hope of rescue. I see no end in sight to the tortuous pleasure and pain. These two sensations seem to blur during his visits. I can't think anymore, and I can't stand it any longer. I have begun to consider the unthinkable because I am too terrified to even think about what sort of creature has me under its control.

What is he? Am I possessed by a demon, the devil, or something even worse? Am I being punished by God? What dire consequences will ensue if I destroy God's gift of life? I can fathom no solution which leaves my soul unscathed. If I permit this abomination to go on, continue as Satan's mistress, I'll be damned for allowing it. If I end my life, I'll be condemned for destroying what God created for me. All I know with certainty is that I must not allow this situation to continue unchanged.

One morning, I have the opportunity, and I finally find the courage to leap out of the tower window. As I fall toward the cobblestones below, which seems to take a long time, I see two beautiful angels flying alongside me. I am surprised that I can see them, and even more surprised that they are here. They tell me I did not need to take this leap, but that they will stay with me, which helps to ease my fear. It occurs to me that if they had showed up a little sooner, like before I jumped, it might have been more helpful.

I stay conscious as I fall, but after I die, I expect there will be nothingness. My hope is that once I am dead, all will be gone and forgotten. I expect to be in a state of non-existence and that will release me from my confusion and my emotional pain. I crave peace and nothingness... but that doesn't happen.

After my death, the angels remain and help me. They counsel, calm, and inform me about what comes next. I am amazed to discover that I am a living spirit and can still remember everything about my life. Everything has continued except my physical body. I still have all the conflicting thoughts and feelings which I thought my death would silence. I realize I have wasted the gift of my life and sacrificed it for little gain; death has not freed me or solved my problems. I still have the challenges I left unsolved. The lessons which I left unlearned in that lifetime will still need to be mastered in another.

Once I understand this, I feel bad for cutting my life short, but I can't see how I could have altered my desperate situation despite the angels' reassurance that there were alternatives. While I was being tortured, I had no idea how to resolve my dilemma, except to eliminate the body he was torturing. I am glad to be temporarily freed from the entity, but since I am responsible for balancing this escape attempt, I sense I will end up facing him again. I hope that when the time comes, the angels will guide me to find the solution I missed this time.

***

CONCLUSIONS:

The memories of the intense sensations which drove me to cut my life short in this past life were more powerful than anything I'd ever experienced. The level of pleasure I'd endured had been at least 10 times stronger than anything I'd felt in the present. But the increased intensity hadn't made it better. With the emotional and spiritual connections absent, I felt abused and tortured. Though the exciting sensations started as delight, they had ended as agonizing pain. Being treated like an object, rather than as a respected person with feelings and value, had turned pleasure into despair. Worst of all, I'd had no control over what he'd done to me, nor had I been able to restrain my body's responses. My weakness, my inability to resist this dark entity, had crushed any hopes I'd had for the future.

Reliving this experience made me wonder if these hidden memories had affected my current life relationships. I always seemed to have high expectations regarding love and attraction. At some level, I believed that, with a suitable partner, people could attain glorious feelings of bliss while making love. I also firmly believed that in order to create a successful and blissful relationship, a few basic elements needed to be present. There had to be some physical attraction, mental compatibility, and an emotional connection. But I, personally, also required a close spiritual bond. These things in common seemed necessary in order to have a close relationship with a loving partner. Maybe some of my attitudes toward love had been influenced by this past lifetime.

My determined attachment to these ideals has made it a challenge for me to create intimacy in my current relationships. Thus far in my present I had found it difficult to be passionate with my intimate partners. Was it a lack of trust? Was there something wrong with me? Maybe there were critical elements that were missing in my present relationships.

This past life had been shocking in so many ways. The desperate traumas of imprisonment, the hopeless despair, being controlled by a shape-shifting dark entity, and suicide, had felt worse than even the most terrifying of nightmares. I had started exploring my past in order to get help with my weight issues. But perhaps these scenes had come up because they related to my present reasons for being overweight. Would things have been different if the bishop had found me less attractive? Would greater body mass have provided me with more strength or protection from the shape shifter? Would anything have protected me from him?

These had been incredibly intense past life memories. Had they not been so clear and tangible, seeing a shape shifter would have seemed more like science fiction than the truth of what I experienced. I had learned that suicide was not a solution, and that there was definitely continuation after death. I had received the help I had asked for from the angels. But I had not been faithful enough to stay in the situation long enough to find the solution. It also seemed there were many more layers of lessons relating to intimacy and relationships that I had yet to uncover.

Questions:

- Why had I not come close to these levels of arousal with present life partners?

- Was I broken or was the trauma from this past life still affecting me?

- Is there a connection between body mass and feeling safe and protected?

Spiritual Skills Present: Clairaudience, Clairtangency, Clairvoyance, Retrocognition

37

Troy

June 18, 1997, 34 yrs.

I'D LEARNED A LOT from the past lives I had seen so far. It had been interesting that family members from my present had not shown up in any of the lifetimes I'd remembered. Five years ago, at the Past Life Seminar, I had reviewed scenes that showed me in relationships with people from my present. Those lifetimes provided me with the clarity I'd asked for and allowed me to release some of my current life pain. I had hoped we would continue to discover more insights during this session...

***

I AM IN THE ANCIENT CITY OF TROY, long before Helen and the Trojan War. I am the son of a powerful man, the King. My father in this lifetime I recognize as my current life father. He is very controlling, a trait which has occasionally shown itself in the present.

In the first scene, father and I are arguing. My father has decided to send troops into Egypt. I tell him that the small contingent he plans to send will not be enough to accomplish the task. Since I command the army and have led our troops successfully through many brutal engagements, I assume he will listen to me and value my opinion. I have fought the

Egyptians before and know we should not underestimate them. He disagrees and sends a small group of my men on without me, intentionally keeping me behind as a punishment for disagreeing with him. News soon comes that our forces have been overwhelmed, boats destroyed, all of my comrades slain.

My father blames me for the deaths of my men and has me put in prison. A master of manipulation, father makes it look like it was my poor decision to send an insufficient contingent of troops to their deaths. Then he claims I stayed behind because I knew my men would be slaughtered. Soon the public doubts me, but my loyal friends and comrades who know my character and trust my abilities stand by me. They plan to help me get released despite the King's wishes, but someone betrays us and gets word to my father.

I later receive a message from him stating that he is planning to release me. With the promise of my freedom secured, my loyal friends openly show their support and my father is able to discover their identities. Once my friends are exposed, he convinces them that I am the one who has been lying and manipulating the situation to my advantage. This deceitful action turns even my most trusted allies against me.

During the session, as I re-experience these past scenes, I'm shocked by the strength of my physical body's reaction. My muscles tighten, and my heart and breathing rates increase as a white-hot ball of rage expands within me. I'm furious at being unjustly imprisoned in a hellhole for my correct assessment of the military situation. Being fed despicable food and foul water, and provided with no light or decent air to breathe, is intolerable and does nothing to diminish my anger. All of my comrades are dead, any remaining allies my father has turned against me. It is a demoralizing, depressing, and infuriating situation which has destroyed my credibility. No one trusts anything I say now. The only possible way I can think of to protest my treatment is to refuse food, but it is weak resistance at best. My hatred, anger, and despair settle into a cold, dark fury at my father's treachery.

Days blend into months, the passage of time indiscernible in my dark cell. My feeble resistance goes unnoticed, and my once vigorous body withers away, though the fire of my indignation burns bright.

Shortly before my death, my father comes down to visit me. I don't know if he truly intends to attempt reconciliation or not. He is shocked at my physical condition. Before my imprisonment, I was strong and agile with all the grace of a prince of Troy. Now I am so different that he barely recognizes me. I am hideous, weak, and sick. Only my voice retains some fragment of familiarity, but even that is strongly laced with bitterness and anger. I am long past the point of being willing to listen to him, or believe anything he tells me. His actions are that of a weak, small man, unwilling to take responsibility for his poor decision. He has so thoroughly convinced himself that I am to blame for all of this. He actually believes his own lies. Nothing changes and I continue in my misery, plotting escape and revenge, until I eventually starve to death.

As the session ends and my focus returns to the present, I still feel tremendous anger and resentment. This is not a normal feeling for me in my current life and personality. To help me, the facilitator tells me to go to my spiritual sanctuary. I visualize myself at the place where I usually meet with my guides, which helps a lot. As I work on releasing these emotions, Master J joins Achaeus and me.

Master J helps with the healing and reminds me that,

> All anger and frustration are self-directed; from you, toward you. Other people act as mirrors to help you, the attributes you like, you tend to see and like in yourself, while the qualities that you don't like in others are usually qualities you don't like in yourself. The characteristics you do not like are the ones you need to work on. Sometimes you do not see that you possess the very qualities you dislike the most. So whenever you see those traits expressed by others, they will continue bothering you until you understand the lesson.

Master J also tells me that people play different parts throughout their various lifetimes. He's trying to help me understand that in the Trojan lifetime, my father was playing the role of the bad guy. My father's stubbornness, his intractability, his cruelty and manipulativeness, were all qualities I despised about my father. But he points out that I also have those qualities in abundance, which is why I had been so furiously angry. I had manipulated my friends to support my attempted escape. I had been stubborn and unmovable. I had never apologized and continued to blame my father for doing this to me. Looking at my role in the situation and taking responsibility for my actions had never occurred to me. Master J's guidance helps me to understand, release, and heal these past traumas and emotions. He also shares with me that the events of my life in Troy connect to my life as an Aztec Doctor.

After my pitiful death in Troy, I'd wanted revenge, which, according to Master J, I could only take against myself. Since

I had chosen and planned the lives I'd experienced to give me opportunities to learn, I had chosen my role as an Aztec doctor so I could exact vengeance on others. But revenge had left me hollow as an empty shell, not filled with the sated sense of satisfaction I had hoped for. In the Aztec life, a different king still controlled my destiny and held my life in his hands. Though I was free to do cruel things to others, I was still a prisoner of my fate. Vengeance wasn't as satisfying as I expected it would be. I was still blaming others for what they did to me, not taking responsibility for the choices I made in my life. The others in my life were playing the parts I had asked them to play. I was shooting my own messengers, the ones who had agreed to bring the bad news. I had asked them to help me with my failed lessons and then blamed them for doing their jobs so well.

CONCLUSIONS:

This lifetime had brought up so much anger it surprised me, but the uprush of unfamiliar emotions made the memories feel powerfully real.

The appearance of my present life father in the past had been revealing. The interactions I had experienced with him at Troy shed new light on some heretofore unfounded attitudes I sometimes had toward my dad in my present life. Master J's help, deeply laden with spiritual truths presented in ways that had brought me clarity, had been invaluable. I was so grateful for his continued presence and help.

I'd heard that people played roles for each other, but I had not thought about how they reflect to us that which we need to see. When Master J had pointed out the similarities between

my actions and those of my father in that lifetime, I was
stunned. Had my father mirrored qualities I despised so I could
recognize them in myself? Had his role actually been to help
me? I had not seen it from that perspective because I'd gotten
so caught up in blaming my father for unjustly punishing me.
Maybe there had been other perspectives I should have taken
into consideration, like my father's position as King and how it
appeared to others when I publicly disagreed with him.

This session had given me much to think about and come
to terms with. In addition to the lessons about anger
and vengeance, the fact that I had starved to death while
imprisoned probably had something to do with my current
weight situation. Another connection, another lesson.

Spiritual Skills Present: Clairaudience, Claircognizance,
Clairempathy, Clairsentience, Clairvoyance, Retrocognition

38

Highway Robbery

June 24, 1997, 34 yrs.

THIS WAS MY FOURTH past life session, and with help, I was getting the hang of the process. We had started off searching for where my struggles with being overweight and unattractive had originated. We had revisited several traumatic situations which likely had an impact. Reliving traumatic events had brought me an awareness of my old emotions and thoughts. I could see that in times of duress, I had declared that if I'd been larger or stronger, I might have been able to protect myself. I had also concluded that being less attractive was to my advantage. And in the lifetime where I'd starved to death, I had decided that, in some circumstances, size, strength and beauty made no difference. I felt like I was seeing patterns emerge.

In this session, we continued our past life journeys in order to discover a way to resolve my current weight issues. It was looking like more than just food, exercise, and rest affected my physical well-being. My body's health seemed linked to my emotional state, my mental balance, and my spiritual understanding. Digging up these painful experiences had uncovered multiple layers of lessons, which seemed to connect back to the body. It looked like if I wanted to resolve this; I was going to have to contend with a multitude of interrelated issues...

***

As this life opens, I see myself as a young boy long ago in England. My family and I are traveling on a road by coach when we are stopped by highwaymen (robbers). My father gets out of the coach and tries to cooperate with them in order to protect us, but they are not interested in talk and they beat him till he is unmoving on the road. Then they drag my mother out of the coach and take her away. I hear her screaming as they hurt her too. I'm confused and don't know what to do. I am horribly frightened and cry uncontrollably.

This scene disturbs me so much that I can no longer continue with the recall of this lifetime. I am so overwhelmed by feelings of fear and helplessness that I am starting to come out of the deep hypnotic state I had attained. The facilitator tells me to send healing to that child self to help release the emotional trauma of this vicious attack. The clairvoyant who is describing the scene says that the guilt and fear I am feeling, because of my inability to stop these people from hurting my family in this past life, connects to my present feelings of helplessness.

He also says this underlying sense of helplessness connects to the feelings I had as a Roman solider. Being a child and having to do what I am told feels very similar to being a soldier and having to follow orders. I have no way to stop the violence and help my parents, just like, as a Roman soldier; there was no way for me to stop the crucifixion. Being unable to do anything but watch people I care about suffer and die brings up terrible feelings of guilt, sadness, and frustration. The fear I feel seems to center on concerns for the personal safety of my family and me, and from not knowing what comes next.

So far, in reviewing my past life experiences, the ease or difficulty of coming to terms with what I see varies greatly. Usually, once my past comes to light, it doesn't take too much effort to reconcile and heal what has long been buried. But this time, I am having a great deal of trouble letting go of the trauma. How can I possibly come to terms with the pain of helplessly watching as my parents are assaulted and murdered in front of me?

Noticing my difficulty, the facilitator tells me that an angel or ascended master will come and help me with it.

After he affirms this, I suddenly see my spirit self in a shadowy forest. The tall trees let only a modicum of sunlight through their canopy of leaves. Their bark is smooth and greyish. I see many forest creatures around too. They seem strangely calm and unafraid of my presence. Even those who are natural enemies are relaxing peacefully together. Toward the center of a clearing, surrounded by many animals, is a large, tall man sitting under one of the trees. This scene reminds me of a picture I have seen in a storybook or of a familiar place I have been. The man is radiating a dazzling light, a beautiful, blue-green teal colored energy.

When he sees me approaching, he greets me warmly with enthusiasm and a wide smile. As I draw near to him, I am astonished at how much joy and playfulness are emanating from him, yet he also exudes a sense of serenity, peace, and love. He reaches toward me and gently places one of his hands against my cheek. His hand is so large that it covers the side of my head and half of my face. From his warm caress, I sense a flow of wonderful healing energy, and the emotional distress I have been feeling begins to ease.

I am so quiet, and still during this spiritual experience, that the facilitator asks me what is happening. When I describe what I am sensing, he tells me that the beautiful being who has been healing and comforting me with the teal-green energy is the ascended Master Buddha. I am stunned, and my shocked reaction elicits a wonderful laugh from Master Buddha. It is such a joyous sound; it fills and uplifts me. He is loving and serene, and so overflowing with life and joy that it bubbles over into laughter that fills the forest, the animals, and me. A short while later, he takes my hand and bids me farewell. Then the colors, the vision and his presence fade.

I am once again back in the office, at the present time, but feeling so much better than before.

What an incredible presence! I feel so nurtured and healed and ready to laugh again. Master Buddha is the second ascended master I've had the blessing of meeting. The energy such a being emanates is unmistakable. The bright beams of light, the essence of pure unconditional love, radiate out from him in all directions. To be near him feels like stepping close to a campfire on a cold night; warm, safe, and comforted. But to feel his gentle touch was extraordinarily reassuring. Nothing I've read or heard of even comes close to what this felt like. To feel such unconditional, loving acceptance is incredible. I have never felt so seen, so loved.

***

CONCLUSIONS:

Because of the healing I received from Master Buddha, this session ended up better than it had started. His help had enabled me to release some of the emotional trauma, which then allowed me to discover why these memories had affected me so strongly. I was so grateful that he had helped me to come to terms with them.

I had felt that sense of frustration and powerlessness in several lifetimes, and in most of them I had responded badly, acted rashly with impatience, without having considered the big picture. I had not been patient, nor had I learned enough self-control to calm down so I could take advantage of the lesson opportunities that were being presented to me by these challenges.

My feelings of powerlessness arose because I'd felt I had no options, though I suppose I could have found them if I had tried harder. Possibilities always existed, though I might not have liked the alternatives.

I learned about possibilities from a Broadway show I saw when I was a teen. The show was about a guy who was trapped in Europe when war broke out. Caught in the middle, he seemed to have no choices, but when his situation looked hopeless, he kept telling himself, "There are always two alternatives." Throughout the play, he faced no-win situations, but instead of giving in to resignation or terror, he consistently looked for the two alternatives he had learned would always be available. Even if they were not great options, there were still *choices*, after all. Interesting how the memory of this play connected so perfectly to this life lesson! Maybe things would have turned out differently in my past or even in my present, if I had used this positive strategy and looked for options.

The scene which had come up in this session was just a small portion of a past life, but it had been highly relevant. A similar incident had occurred in my present life childhood when my parents had a disagreement about whose turn it was to have us kids. My father had dragged away and hurt my mother. I had felt helpless and afraid in the present, just as I had in the past. The two incidents eerily echoed each other. My fear, guilt, and frustration had created a sense of uncertainty and insecurity within me. This present-life connection must have been why I had become so emotionally upset and couldn't go on. Thank goodness I had received help with healing this piece of my history. I hoped it would relieve my uncertainty and insecurity in both lifetimes.

In this session, it had also become apparent that some past lives were intense, and contained lessons which still needed to be learned, and it would be necessary to revisit them several times to get to all the layers and emotions. For this session, I could not have gone on or handled any more than I had.

With each recall, release of emotions, and reflection on the lessons learned, my perspective had changed. Each time I dealt with my past, I noticed different things and got into deeper layers. I would have to trust the facilitator, the clairvoyant and my higher self to know when I needed to take another deeper look, and also when it was time to move on to the next lesson.

Spiritual Skills Present: Clairaudience, Claircognizance, Clairempathy, Clairsentience, Clairtangency, Clairvoyance, Divine timing, Energy Healing, Intuition, Retrocognition

39

Kidnapped!

July 13, 1997, 34 yrs.

So far, I had received some answers which had begun to explain my abhorrence of violence and the difficulties I had in losing weight. The facilitator and clairvoyant guiding my regression work had said I would have answers to my weight-loss challenges within six sessions. That highly motivated me to get my sessions scheduled so that I could work through what needed to be done.

Doing one session a week had been tough. The last session had struck some really deep emotions, so I had needed more time to process what had been uncovered. But now, I was ready for the next step of my journey...

I am a young girl, maybe eight or nine years old. My younger brother and I are playing outside when a couple of men drive by and kidnap us. They are cruel and twisted. The men blindfold us before taking us to a run-down, abandoned house that seems to be in the middle of nowhere. They put my brother into another room of the house. The windows are so filthy that they are nearly opaque, and paint is peeling off the walls of the place. I know the back of the house faces east because the morning sun tries to shine through the back windows of the dining room, while dimmer light comes in from the south down the hall from the bedroom windows.

They tie my hands with cloth rags. I keep insisting that I want to see my brother. My brother needs to be with me. I need to see if he is okay. He should be with me. He is younger than me and probably even more scared than I am.

I think the kidnappers know it will be harder on us both being separated. That is probably why the men are doing it. They seem to enjoy the pain they are causing us. Keeping us isolated works well for them. They take me down the hall once during our captivity and show me my brother. They have bound him, hands and feet, and he is lying on a bed in one of the back rooms. He is pale, weak and clearly frightened. All I have time to say is, "It's gonna be all right, Jeffrey." Then they march me back down the hall to the dining room and make me sit in that hard chair again.

Time passes, days, I think. I am so hungry. They have not fed me much: a bit of a wafer, a crust of bread and some cheese. I'm hungry but I can manage. I am worried about my little brother.

They won't let me see him, even though I keep asking about him. I don't want to ask for food again. They seem to like it when I beg for food. I feel so hungry. The days seem endless, and time seems to run all together. I can't tell how much time has passed. I am weak from lack of nourishment and sore from sitting in the hard chair so much.

Finally, one day I can smell food cooking. I am so hungry that I break down and ask for something to eat. They bring me something. It looks like strips of meat. It looks good, and I am starving—really hungry. I hope my brother is getting some food too. I hope they have been feeding my brother enough. I would gladly give him my food if necessary.

But something feels wrong. I have not heard a sound from my brother in a long time. I tell the kidnappers I have to see him. They agree I can see him after I eat lunch.

Something tells me that there is something wrong with my brother. I can just tell. As I chew on the meat, the feeling grows stronger. I have been watching my captors. They aren't eating; they are just watching me. Once in a while, they give each other a weird look, and then laugh.

I stop between bites and ask them what kind of meat this is. We live on a farm and I have tried all sorts of meat parts, but this is different. As they laugh at my question. My feelings of dread increase.

"You wanted to see your brother... well, there he is," they say as they point to my plate. Then they laugh even louder at my reaction.

My revulsion is supreme. I am horrified and nauseous. I throw up and cry harder than I ever have before. Oh my God, how could these men be so brutal and heartless? My mind races as I think about what is in store for me, and I realize I might not live through this to see my family, the farm, and my friends again. After my initial panic, my pain and anguish settle into a cold, heartless fury. At the next opportunity, I will use every ounce of my strength to escape.

***

CONCLUSIONS:

During and after the session, I had broken down and cried hard. These had been very challenging scenes to recall. After the initial shock, my feelings of anger, disgust, and sorrow had taken a while to subside. It had been terrible to look at, and it was even harder to accept. The facilitator had asked that I receive help from spirit with processing and releasing the trauma. This very unpleasant association of food, starvation, and violence felt like it was definitely related to my current weight situation.

This session had been very shocking to me, and it took a long time for me to learn to accept the events I'd remembered. Few things were more disturbing than what I'd experienced.

Questions:

- Had I kept the extra weight on in order to feel more powerful?

- Had I become large so that I would not be easy prey for kidnappers or be a victim again?

- Had I gained weight in my current life during a time when I felt vulnerable and in need of protection?

- Would the weight finally come off when I felt safe and protected?

Spiritual Skills Present: Clairaudience, Claircognizance, Clairsentience, Clairvoyance, Intuition, Retrocognition

40

Lake Déjà vu & Southwest Flash flood

July 20, 1997, 34 yrs.

SOMETIMES TROUBLES OF THE PAST overflowed into the present. At this, my sixth session, the facilitator asked me if I had any recurring nightmares. I told them that there were two recurring nightmares which I had endured during childhood, my teenage years, and even occasionally as an adult. (see Chapter 1). The fear these terrifying dreams created each time they occurred hadn't diminished over the years.

We decided to look into these incidents to see if we could get any answers which connected to the present...

***

I DESCRIBE THE FIRST recurring nightmare to the facilitators. It is the one about me being trapped in my bathroom with the toilet overflowing. I am about to drown when I wake up screaming. As the clairvoyant and I go into this memory, we trace it to a past life event.

I am a young child, a boy, I think, but gender doesn't seem to be important. My family and I are out on a boat in the middle of a lake, cooling off on a hot summer afternoon. I'm not sure if we are fishing or just on an outing. Being on the lake is a cooler place in the summertime than being on dry land. I feel like I am somewhere near large expanses of prairies, a mostly hot and dry region.

I don't know if it's 'cause I'm leanin' too far over the side while I'm looking at the water or if I just get bumped, but I fall in. I don't know how to swim, and the water envelops me as I slowly sink till I am about ten to twenty feet below the surface. I look up from deep under the water and can see the sun shining through. It looks so beautiful! But I don't see anyone diving in tryin' to save me. I don't think they know I fell in yet.

The facilitator assumes I am frightened, struggling, panicking and fearful. I'm not. It's so quiet down here. I feel like time is standing still as I hang suspended in the cool water. It feels like I can almost breathe the water and be just fine, like a fish. I am very relaxed and filled with a sense of peace.

It is some length of time before my family notices that I'm not on the boat. By then, things start fading for me. I'm not scared, but I feel like I am falling asleep. Then things go dark. I guess I pass out or drown.

+ + +

This past life memory connects to my first recurring nightmare, the water-filled bathroom. Funny that the dream I've been experiencing is so frightening, yet my actual death seems rather peaceful. It's weird that my fearful dream is scarier than my death. Why is that? Where do nightmares come from? Do these dreams originate from within me, or are they caused by something outside of me?

Perhaps my family's emotional anguish in response to my death relates to my bad dreams in the present. I have heard that the energy of people's grief can delay the progress of a spirit. Lots of sad emotions can create a fog or thread-like tendrils of energy, which can slow or keep the soul from moving on. If my prior life family's feelings created that kind of energy and are connected to me, maybe those energies strengthen my recurring nightmares.

I also wonder if this past lifetime connects to the "Déjà View" incident I had experienced while visiting a roadside market when I was 10 years old. I had been on a road trip with Aunt Dottie and Uncle Joe. The market we had stopped at had been surrounded by fields as far as the eye could see. I hope clarity would come in time if it needed to.

+ + +

THE SECOND RECURRING NIGHTMARE relates to a rolling ball of adobe that chases me and almost runs me over. This rolling ball of reddish mud behaves like one of those cartoon snowballs rolling downhill, collecting more and more dirt as it gets closer to me. By the end of the nightmare, the ball is taller than a house and has sticks, straw and debris sticking out all over it. I can never run fast enough to get away from it, and even if I dodge it, it follows me. Just before it crushes me, I wake up screaming. The worst part is that, once it starts, it keeps repeating every time I go back to sleep. When the dream sequence starts over again, I try even harder to evade it, but I still can't get away.

We discover another past life connection as we search for the cause of the adobe ball nightmare. This time, I am a Native American of the Southwestern United States. Several children and I are down in the creek tending to our daily activities of washing, bathing, and getting water. A short distance away, a storm is brewing, and the skies are darkening. We are finishing our chores when someone from the village comes to warn us to move away from the creek and seek shelter and safety. The storm is moving more swiftly than expected.

We get most of the children to run to a safe place on higher ground, but a very young child is still dawdling by the creek bed. I go down to get her when I hear a rumbling. The ground starts to shake. I look up to see an enormous wave of water and mud crashing through the creek bed. I grab the child and duck behind one of the boulders near the edge of the creek. As the first wave slams by, the boulder shelters us and keeps us protected. I am able to step up and hand the child to another adult before another wall of liquid mud cascades over the top of the boulder. Sand and debris are crashing down on me, a waterfall of reddish-brown, straw-laden mud. I can't breathe. It's so heavy. I'm caught between two boulders and the incoming flow of heavy mud traps me there. I am terrified, panic-stricken, and suffocating in the liquefied earth. Unable to free myself, I drown, trapped between the boulders.

This death experience is worse than my nightmare.

***

CONCLUSIONS:

After this session, my nightmares never returned. By recalling the two lifetimes, I was able to understand and release the fear and trauma of those events. I'd also received some insights as to why I've had breathing problems in my present life. My current physical ailments seemed to have had their beginnings in other lifetimes. When I died being unable to breathe, it left some residual trauma, which affected my lungs in the present. Perhaps I had not learned the lessons offered by these experiences or released the emotions connected to them. Refusing to accept the unacceptable situations of the past could keep the energies lingering in my present. Left unresolved, they would eventually express themselves as disease. Once I understood, accepted and released the past, I hoped that my current symptoms would improve.

I was grateful that I finally had answers to this lifelong mystery. Not only had my nightmares stopped, but now I knew they had been reflections of actual events, not just figments of my imagination. My subconscious had created dreams that eventually helped me to release these past traumas and heal.

The sessions had also brought the gift of other memories, which were much more pleasant. The experiences of the peace and quiet I'd felt when I was under the water, and the marvelous feelings of how close I had been to my family on the lake, were beautiful and special. I had also felt a strong sense of community with my tribe and a deep connection to the children of the village. It was wonderful knowing that I had been able to save that last child.

Spiritual Skills Present: Clairaudience, Claircognizance, Clairempathy, Clairsentience, Clairvoyance, Retrocognition

41

The Farmer's Daughter

July 27, 1997, 35 yrs.

IN THIS SESSION, WE delved into the subject of loving relationships.
I'd not had much success in this area of my current life. I
hoped that we would discover clues to help me improve in my
present...

***

IT FEELS LIKE I AM living in a Puritan settlement. It is really
green in our area, with lots of trees that turn bright colors
in the fall. I live with my father and mother. I am a young
lady of marriageable age. My parents are currently considering
candidates for a marriage arrangement for me. I object to this.
I don't like any of the men they have selected so far, and my
prospects seem dim.

One hot and humid afternoon, I am sitting out in the barn, up
in the hayloft. My friend is here visiting with her family today
and we chat about our current situations. We commiserate
together about the process we are both enduring right
now—arranged marriages set up by our parents. We both feel
afraid of what may lie ahead for us, and we try to comfort each
other as best we can. Sitting next to my friend in the hay, I feel
a connection and a sudden, surprising attraction to her.

Conversation flows effortlessly from topic to topic between us, and drifts to talk about intimate experiences we have had. To my delight and dismay, she says she feels drawn to me right now too. We touch each other hesitantly and finally share a kiss of such tenderness that I feel a strong uprush of feelings and sensations. That it was beyond amazing barely describes the experience. It feels like nothing I have ever felt with any of my other suitors. It was like a spiritual experience, a sense of knowing, in my heart, mind and soul. We don't do more than kiss, but it is as if we connect on a soul level. The strength of our feelings is frightening.

A relationship of this nature is not possible in our society, so we decide not to spend any more time alone together. We plan to spend time apart to allow us to forget this accidental attraction. We want to get on with our lives and live the lives our families expect us to, the lives we have grown to expect for ourselves.

Months pass, and I am missing my friendship with her. I keep busy with my chores and my parents' chosen suitors, trying not to think about my friend too much. But sometimes, when I am in the hayloft, I think about what happened between us. I wonder if I imagined my attraction to her. But when I picture us kissing, my body swiftly and strongly responds, and it doesn't seem like imagination. Remembering makes me feel worse, so I decide to stay away from the loft as much as I can. I must stop feeling like this!

My parents are growing impatient with my moping around and gently pressure me to choose a husband. When I marry, it will ease my parents' emotional and financial concerns about me. I feel confused and indecisive. I dislike the men my parents have selected for me and we quarrel.

Crying, I run out to the hayloft to be alone with my sorrows. I curl up in the hay and am crying for a while before I realize I am not alone. My friend is here! We hug and talk for what feels like a long, long time. She has missed me too and has been worrying about me. She sneaked away from home to come to the loft, hoping for the chance to see me should I come out here.

After some initial discomfort, we talk about what happened between us months ago. Neither of us wants to feel this powerful attraction. Both of our families plan to marry us off soon, but neither of us are interested in the suitors they have chosen for us. I want so very much to like one of the gentleman candidates.

Keeping an open mind, I socialize with them when they are here to dine. I sit and talk with them on the porch, and a few of them I've allowed to kiss me. When I do, I expect that wonderful surge of attraction and connection with them, just like it happened with my friend. But it just doesn't happen. Their kisses feel lifeless and boring. Yet now, just sitting here talking with my dear friend, all my senses come alive and I feel connected to her. My soul is vibrant, tingling with energy and awareness. My body longs to be touching her and to be touched by her.

Unable to resist such powerful feelings, we soon draw together, tentatively at first, then clinging desperately and passionately to each other. I feel safe and loved within her arms. I have never felt like this with anyone else, so close to another human being, as I do with her at this moment. We stop all too soon, fearful that someone will come looking for us. Together, in our own world, we have completely lost track of how long we've been out here. Time flows differently when we are together. Sometimes moments feel like days, other times hours feel like moments. We decide to meet later, in a more private place, so we can figure out what to do next.

In a secluded clearing in the woods, we meet to discuss our situation. As we talk things out, we discover that both of us resolutely know that we want to please and help our families. We decide to go along with our respective families' marriage arrangements and agree to never meet again.

The separation is difficult to bear. Even my mother notices my sadness. I desperately wish that I could explain to my parents what is happening within me, but I don't understand it myself and wouldn't know how to explain it to someone else.

Time crawls tortuously by. It's clear to me now that the feelings I have for my friend are much deeper than I originally thought. I love her at such a deep level; it is impossible to explain it as anything but a spiritual or soul connection.

She is just as miserable as I am. On rare occasions, we pass each other in the marketplace and nod politely, savoring every moment of eye contact. But I don't dare to spend more than a few moments near her, for fear that my feelings will show. I know I cannot speak to her without betraying myself, and so I avoid all conversation. My mother notices me keeping my distance from my friend and remarks on it later that evening. I give her a lame explanation, but I can tell Mother is suspicious.

One afternoon, I see my friend at the market and quietly whisper a message to her. My family will all be away from home this afternoon, and we can be alone. It's a chance for me to talk to her privately, to let her know that my affianced husband is planning for us to move far away after we wed. I have to let her know. I have to be with her one last time, to say goodbye in private.

We meet in the loft as usual. When I see her and feel her presence, my words freeze in my mouth, but our bodies can't remain apart any longer. We kiss and love each other so joyfully, so happy to be together, even for a short time. We talk softly as we make love, whispering endearments, gentle words between kisses. I tell her of my upcoming move and marriage, that if left up to me, I would choose to be with her forever.

Unbeknownst to us, my parents have come home earlier than expected. They have overheard us. We freeze in fear when they make their presence known. They ask us to come into the house. We sit in the living room, and my mother relates what they've overheard. My father is terribly upset, though my mother seems less surprised. She explains we cannot continue as we have been doing.

If people find out what we've done, we will be excommunicated, and then executed. Our actions are considered sinful and sacrilegious—a heresy against God. But my mother has seen how unhappy I've been during the time my friend and I have been apart. She also heard the joyful contentment in my voice while my friend and I were together in the loft. My mother sincerely wants me to be happy since she has not had that kind of joy in her life, except for the time we've spent together as mother and daughter. She feels that the love and joy that blooms between people comes from God. Somehow my mother convinces my father to allow us to leave.

There is a rustic hunting cabin which my father sometimes uses in winter located far away from town. My parents let us go to live there. Life is a daily struggle to survive, but at least we are together. This is remarkably kind and tolerant of my parents. I guess I have been underestimating and under-appreciating them. They are quite remarkable, and I am grateful for their concern for my happiness.

My partner and I have some precious time together at the cabin. But our joy is short-lived. Her parents are not so forgiving, and her brothers have been searching for our hiding place. They find us and drag us back to the village where people mock us and throw objects at us. After a quick, unjust trial, they condemn us to death for heresy. We are each tied, hands and neck to a long pole and marched down the main road through town, thoroughly and publicly humiliated before being brutally executed.

CONCLUSIONS:

This session was shocking to me on many levels. The clarity of what I experienced made me reconsider my opinions about love, gender, and my ability to receive information from Spirit. The intensity and depth of my feelings and the specific details were hard to discount. My life with my parents, the short blissful time my friend and I had together, the trauma of our final hours and our execution had all been quite vivid and very disturbing. Had I been shown these experiences so that I could broaden my definition of love? Perhaps I'd needed to feel the intense connection between my friend and me so I could understand how soul love defies the limitations of human perspective.

It had been absolutely clear in this past life that I desperately wanted to cooperate with my family and community. But inner conflicts arose when I had to decide between following the urgings of my heart and soul and doing what my family expected. I was not trying to be rebellious, disobedient, or commit heresy against my God. But the energy and love I'd felt for my friend was so strong that I hadn't been able to stop myself. Suppressing my feelings had been like trying to hold back a river. I had tried so hard, but my emotions had still broken through every barrier. It was sad to be executed for loving someone. We had been harming no one, yet we were considered criminals.

The topics that had come up in this session motivated me to learn more about the attraction between people. It was clear in that lifetime that more than physical appearance was involved in bringing my friend and me together. There seemed to have been an intractable force between us. We also had mental and emotional compatibility, and an intuitive understanding of each other. Every time we had tried to stay away from each other, something had drawn us back together again. It was something we could not explain or ignore.

Many would call this unmistakable response to another person chemistry. But I think the chemistry of attraction involves more than just a physical reaction. The connection between my friend and me had been strengthened by our easy friendship, compatible beliefs, and mutually intense feelings. There had also been plenty of other feelings urging me to do as my parents had taught me. I loved and honored my parents. I felt deeply connected to God, my community, and our traditional ways. It had never been my intention to hurt or upset my family, nor had I wished to betray my beliefs, or upset my friends. Yet, the connection that existed between my friend and I had been so strong, the bond we shared had made all other emotions pale in comparison. The only feeling in my present life which came close to what I'd felt for my friend was the unconditional loving presence of Master Jesus. His presence had been the strongest force I had ever felt until this regression experience.

When such potent energy flowed between two people, there seemed to be no way to deny or resist it. Our connection had felt uplifting and gentle, kind and supportive, all-knowing, all-accepting, and all-loving, an extension of the unconditional love that God himself bestows upon us all. It was as if a spark of the Divine had flowed within and between us, and could be tapped into. Perhaps every soul could bring in and express that loving power.

From a higher perspective, lessons felt like we had chosen them, not only for my friend and me, but for all who had been there and had interacted with us. It had been a demonstration that love between beings cannot be measured or limited by man's feeble understanding of love. Our love had a transcendent quality which the dissenting opinions and thoughts of others could not diminish. Even the conflicts within us were not strong enough to suppress its pure quality. A true spiritual connection, love between souls, was much deeper than the superficial understanding of it by many humans on earth. Few could even imagine the possible depths.

After recalling this experience, I knew what kind of loving connection could and had existed on earth for my friend and myself, however briefly. It was reassuring to know that I was capable of this kind of deep love. The intense emotions I had experienced, I would not soon forget.

Spiritual Skills Present: Clairaudience, Clairempathy, Clairsentience, Clairvoyance, Divine timing, Retrocognition

42

Not so Holy...

August 4, 1997, 35 yrs.

THE WEIGHT ISSUES had not been resolved within six sessions, as estimated. The traumas we'd looked at had been intense and had affected my thoughts, beliefs, emotions, relationships, *and* the physical body. I'd had no idea there were so many overlapping components contributing to my health and well-being. With so much involved, it wasn't surprising that there were many more pieces of the puzzle to locate before I would get to the core of this issue.

I hoped we would find a few more pieces in this session...

Author's Note: Disturbing violence of a sexual nature occurred frequently in the following lifetime. There is also some involvement with a religious group, the details of which I have kept as generic as possible, primarily to provide a framework for my experience. The situations, relationships, and lesson opportunities are the primary focus of this lifetime.

***

AS WE TUNE INTO this lifetime, I sense that I am a young woman, alone, with no family or support system. It feels like I am living somewhere in Europe, possibly Spain, centuries ago. Every day is a struggle to survive, and to find honest work. I have a room with few possessions. Desperate, starving, with nowhere else to turn, I end up selling my body in order to support myself.

I am quite religious, so the inner conflict wreaks havoc with my morals and self-esteem. My feelings of guilt and self-loathing expand each time I am forced to receive a customer, and I am very concerned about my immortal soul. Some clients are brutally cruel, causing injuries that make me question the risk, but with the options I have, I must either risk injury or die of starvation. My body is young and strong and I recover quickly, though soon enough I develop a sense of who is likely to be vicious, and try to avoid them. I have to do what I must in order to survive. I continue to seek legitimate work, but as what I do becomes more widely known, fewer decent people even speak to me.

I spend a lot of time in the nearby church. I stay in the back, out of sight, praying for forgiveness and help from God. A miracle would be wonderful, but I have little hope of that. Sometimes while I am there, the choir sings. Their beautiful voices sound so angelic. They sing a lot of chants, and it echoes off the walls of the church through my heart and soul. During times like these, I feel almost human, deserving and hopeful again.

After some good fortune, I am able to buy a dress nice enough to go to church in. This allows me to go to confession, which is a balm for my soul. I cannot explain everything to the priest, but I feel God knows the entire story and will understand.

There are several priests at my church, overseen by an older bishop. Often, one of the young priests helps in confession. One in particular is very kind, soft-spoken, and quite handsome. I am drawn to him, mostly to his gentle manner and the kind, respectful way he talks to me. It is quite different treatment than what I usually receive from men.

Months go on and I often see the young Priest in my weekly visits to the confessional. We become friends, comfortable and glad to be in each other's company. After one particularly vicious client beats me badly, I cannot go to church for several weeks, and I am missed. My young Priest friend has been asking around the neighborhood about me. I am evidently rather striking in appearance, so I am known to my neighbors.

The Priest finds me. I am in my room, bruised, feverish, dehydrated and delirious. He takes care of my immediate needs and then gets someone to look after me. When he visits a few days later, I am doing much better, sitting up having some soup. I am glad to see him, but feel sad and ashamed to tell him the truth about how I got hurt. He sits with me and is very sympathetic, understanding the reality that sometimes life offers few choices of direction. Moved by my situation, he leans over and gently touches my face with his hand, a gesture of compassion. But something passes between us at this moment. I can see it in his face. He quickly withdraws his hand, not looking me in the eye afterwards.

Time passes and I recover and return to church. My priest friend has paid for my lodging for some time, so I can survive without selling myself, while I continue to look for honest work. I express to him my gratitude for his and the church's support during a confession session.

The next big event in my life occurs when my priest friend has a personal crisis. I am at confession and describe to him my dismay at having to resume the occasional sale of my body to keep me alive. As I ask for God's help and strength to endure, my friend becomes upset and starts crying. I ask him what is wrong, but he is incoherent. I ask him to meet me at my lodging, away from church, so we can talk privately. He agrees to meet me.

My priest friend arrives looking sad and desolate. His bishop has sexually abused him. He is physically hurt, but the emotional and spiritual damage is even more severe. The bishop's act of violence has deeply shaken his faith in the teachings of his church. He doubts his judgement of everything he once held dear, his reverence for the bishop, even his regard and trust in the other priests. I hold and comfort him for a long time until he falls asleep.

I bring him food when he awakens. He is much calmer. I hug him, and when we draw apart, we hesitate and then kiss. We didn't plan it, but there is a strong connection and attraction between us. I have never felt attracted to anyone before, and he hasn't either. Feelings and energy quickly envelop us before we are even aware of what is happening. As we realize what we are doing, we jump apart, each of us apologizing to the other. After this incident, I try to avoid him, not wanting to get either of us in trouble with God or the church. I make sure I do my confessions with one of the other priests. I avoid him successfully for several months, but eventually he ends up with me at my confession because no one else is available.

I don't go into detail about what has been happening in my life. His words are polite and distant. He seems hollow and sad, and he tells me he misses my friendship. I miss his friendship just as much. He quietly tells me that the bishop's abuses have continued and that he can do nothing to stop them. My priest friend says he has been told that if he tells anyone about the abuse, he will lose his position. He could even be excommunicated or killed. I wish I knew how to help him, but all I can do is offer my support and sympathy.

Another month passes before my priest friend unexpectedly comes to see me. Miserable and lonely, we fall into each other's arms and love each other. I love him. I have never had these feelings for anyone else, and he feels the same about me. This is a great sin in the eyes of the church, but when we are together, it doesn't feel like a sin. The abuses he is enduring seem so much worse to both of us. As much as we might wish it, he cannot stay here with me. We will both be in terrible trouble if they find out about us. So, too soon, he goes back to the church and far away from me.

Not long afterwards, the bishop calls me into his office. I don't know how, but he knows about the love my priest friend and I have for each other. I am terrified. The bishop promises to destroy my friend's career, his life, unless he receives sexual favors from me. It is blackmail, and the bishop will be coming to see me.

The day comes. This bishop is cruel and vicious, more so than any of my other clients. The surface damage he does, I can conceal with my clothing, but the psychological and emotional cruelty of this man is far worse than anyone I have ever met. His male body part is the most enormous I have ever seen. I am stunned and fearful. Even though I have been with large men, this is more than my body is used to. He starts his penetration slowly, but nothing can prevent the tearing I feel as he mercilessly forces himself into me. I scream and pass out.

I wake up later, bloodied and traumatized, but thankfully, the bishop is gone. I take quite a while to heal from his physical abuse, but the emotional damage I will never recover from.

Later, I find out that he told my neighbors, as an explanation for my screams, that he was exercising demons from me. People treat me differently after that, sort of wary and nervous. I am different. No longer do I search for legitimate work. I feel so damaged in every way after that. I am broken, depressed, and hopeless.

When I am able, I return to church. My continued presence is one of the bishop's blackmail conditions. I am called in again to his office. This time, my beloved priest friend is there, kneeling on the floor. The bishop informs us he has heard whispers, and that we are going to be punished. I am sure neither of us has said anything, so it feels like this is just an excuse. He has us taken to a special room, private, somewhere down in the deepest bowels of the church.

The room has thick stone walls, so no sound escapes. Assistants help with preparations for the Bishop's sadistic pleasures. There is a stone table which they chain me to. Nearby, they force my priest friend into a vulnerable position, and he is also bound. He abuses both of us; though for me it feels worse to hear my friend cry out in pain and humiliation, than to feel the piercing cruelness of the bishop's body and the sting of his vicious taunts. He seems like the epitome of evil to me. The darkness of his soul is frightening.

He allows us time to heal, and then has us brought before him again, sometimes at the same time, sometimes separately. One day, when we find a few minutes to speak privately, we plan to run away together. We can see no other solution. We cannot ask someone in authority or anyone else for help. Who would believe us?

Unfortunately, the bishop discovers our plan and is furious. He has us brought to his chamber of horrors, and he unleashes the full force of his wrath upon us. This time, he adds stabbing wounds with ceremonial daggers to his abuses. He kills my love first, while I am forced to watch. I am next.

The small stab wounds add to the pain, but cause little bleeding. I think the bishop does it to keep me focused on the pain. But after my pain reaches a certain level, I feel almost numb. I did not know how much he had been holding back until I feel the damage being done to me now. I know I will not survive this and feel gratitude when death finally welcomes me.

CONCLUSIONS:

This lifetime had a profound emotional impact on me during the experience and when I recalled these events. Trust had been one of the major issues of that lifetime. I had believed that I could get legitimate work. I had faith that if I was a good person and did the right things, then God would protect and support me in my efforts to live a decent life. Yet I had not felt supported by God during most of that life. I had felt deceived. I had prayed for God to help me, yet I'd been forced to sell myself or die of starvation. Somehow, I had survived, but then felt progressively less worthy of God's respect and love. By the end of my life, the bishop's selfish, vile acts overpowered and destroyed any faith I had left. The church leader that I'd trusted the most to aide, protect, and inspire me had turned out to be the one I could trust the least.

Had my faith been misplaced in the officials, the teachings, and the institution that I should have been able to rely on? In that life, I had attended church faithfully, prayed daily, listened intently to the messages of the church leadership, and had

done my best to abide by the laws of my faith and society.
Yet I was so desperately poor that it had been necessary to
sacrifice my morals and self-respect to feed myself. Could
the church have been more supportive, helped me find work,
or provided me with sustenance until I could sustain myself?
Their teachings spoke of such things, yet their actions spoke
otherwise.

I had received spiritual guidance and kindness from my Priest
friend. God sent him to help me when I was injured, near death.
But if I had received help earlier, then perhaps it wouldn't have
been necessary to put myself in the risky situation that had
caused the injuries.

Could these past life experiences, the negativity and trauma,
have connections to my current doubts and fears? I've
had a long-held mistrust of people in authority, especially
males. Maybe my doubts about organized religion had their
beginnings in this past life. In my current life, I had
sought guidance and explored many religions. But my search
always ended in disappointment because I never received
straightforward answers to my questions. Nor did I receive
any solace from their teachings. Some of these churches
had welcomed me and offered some small support—at first.
But always, at a certain point, I found that their support
was withdrawn or became conditional. Support would only
continue if I paid their price of obedience and tithing.

My present attitudes toward sex and love were likely
influenced by this past life. Then, sex had become a commodity,
an act without emotion or spirit. When feelings of love had
arisen between my priest friend and me, things had changed
and sex became an uplifting experience. With him, it was joyful
and spiritually expansive. In my present, I have steadfastly

believed that there had to be a spiritual component to love and sex or it felt empty, without meaning. I hadn't known when or where that attitude had come from, only that I'd always felt strongly about it.

In my present life, I also tended to be uncomfortable with male attention and downplayed any focus on my beauty and physical appearance. Maybe being overweight had become a way of staying unattractive. Perhaps my present issues with weight also connected to my feelings of scarcity from my lack of food and my lack of comfort and protection. I had believed in God so deeply. But I had also felt betrayed by the apparent lack of support from the Holy ones whom I loved so much.

There seemed to be some past/karmic connections regarding relationships connected to this life. While reviewing this lifetime, I recognized that my priest friend was someone I had loved in my present (CK). Seeing this past life expanded my understanding of the connection we had in my current life. He had been the same angry soldier who had cut off my hands when I fell off a cliff. This time he fell for me as my priest friend and lost his life, and in our other past life, I fell and lost my life. When he fell for me as a priest, it was a spiritual misstep, and when I fell and ignored the advice of my guardian angel, it was also a spiritual misstep, a lack of trust. These incidences and lifetimes had felt related on a deep level, but I wasn't sure why or how I knew that.

Perhaps I had experienced these situations just so I would know what they felt like. Maybe some life events could only be truly comprehended by actually living them. Only first-hand experience, with all the nuances and feelings, could provide a thorough understanding. Some encounters were so powerful on so many levels that effectively describing them with words was nearly impossible.

Questions:

- Did the soul choose lifetimes to create fears and traumas and then choose experiences to have opportunities to overcome them?

- Was it my choice to endure poverty, starvation, sexual assault, and murder? Or were these traumas some sort of balancing action for my prior wrongdoings in other lifetimes?

Spiritual Skills Present: Clairaudience, Claircognizance, Clairempathy, Clairsentience, Clairvoyance, Retrocognition

43

On my Own

August 29, 1997, 35 yrs.

THE SUMMER OF 1997 had been distressing because of changes that had occurred within the spiritual group I'd been attending. Up to this point, two people had been helping guide my regression sessions. One person acted as the facilitator, who directed the sequence of the session while staying present and alert. The other person, the clairvoyant, went into an intuitive trance and described scenes, spirit presences, energies and other details they sensed.

But now, because of the changes, there would no longer be a clairvoyant available to help with the regression sessions. I would have to learn to trust what I could sense on my own. But I wasn't a psychic! This was something I wasn't sure I could do. My goal was to keep digging into my past to get help with my present challenges. I hoped that somehow, with the facilitator's guidance, I could continue my journey...

***

AS I GO INTO the meditation part of the session, I am surprised to find myself being guided by my higher self into a past life. I am a young woman in my 20s, in a troubled relationship. My husband is mentally, emotionally, and physically abusive. We are arguing again and I know how it's going to end. I don't want to deal with the violence anymore. I'm through with being beaten and treated like dirt. So, when he turns his back and is intent on his work, I quietly slip out and flee into the nearby woods. My goal is to get far enough ahead of him so I can hide. I need to get away, to find a safe place where no one will hurt me anymore.

Unfortunately, he catches up to me, beats me severely, then rapes me and leaves me for dead. When I regain consciousness, I am lying on the forest floor. I am filthy. A mixture of blood, dirt, and tattered clothing clings to my skin. Part of me wishes I didn't wake up. By sheer strength of will, I get my body up and moving. I must get out of here. I know my husband will return. Having me around to use as a punching bag for taking out his frustrations is a convenience he will want to keep under his control. He has the legal right to do anything he wants to me, and the power enthralls him. He will definitely be back.

My fear urges me to pull myself together and stumble on through the forest to find a safe haven away from my husband. I don't know where I am going. I have never gone very far from home, so I have no idea how much time passes or where I am. Nearing exhaustion and barely conscious, I come into a clearing on what must be the other side of the forest. Through blurring eyes, I can see a small house and farm. There is a man hard at work plowing his field. I am still quite disoriented. He looks up, sees me, and then everything goes black again.

I wake up to find myself clean and well taken care of. Every part of my body seems to ache with pain. The man I saw in the field is here. I am frightened, yet somehow I know I am safe. He gently cares for me, and though we don't speak the same language, we seem to understand each other. I don't say too much and he is a quiet sort of man, much different from my husband.

This man is somehow familiar and so very kind. He lives on this small farm with his young son. It seems that his wife died when his son was born. As I grow strong again, we get to know each other and I help him with his farm and his son. We get along very well together, working side-by-side, content with companionable silence or gentle words. I am anxious, though. I know my husband will come looking for me.

Soon enough, as predicted, my vicious husband comes out of the woods one day on the same forest path I had found. I am in the little house when he arrives. When I see him, I panic. The kind man understands and hides me in a trunk. Frozen in fear, I pray my husband will go away and give up searching for me. The kind man goes out to meet my spouse, drawing him away from the house. My vicious husband, unable to communicate with my kind friend, quickly gives up his search in disgust and goes back from whence he came.

We keep a vigilant watch for him for some time after that. But thankfully, my vicious husband never returns. He has probably found someone new to terrorize.

I stay on to help the kind man. We grow to love each other very much. It is such a different relationship than what I was in before. What we have is so respectful, loving, gentle and passionate, much better than what it was like with my first husband. We eventually marry and enjoy a happy life together.

CONCLUSIONS:

I was so grateful that I had been able to tune into my past without the presence of a clairvoyant! The facilitator had guided me into a meditative or trance state and then had given me instructions along the way. It sometimes felt as if I had been making scenes up out of my imagination, but then, when the emotions rushed in, it all became incredibly real.

What I sensed felt valid because of the emotions which had come up. I had released some of the stuck emotional energy and forgiven my former spouse for his vicious behavior. He actually made it possible for me to find a truer happiness than I'd had with him. It seemed like I had experienced a lot of lifetimes where abuse was prevalent. I hoped I would eventually find out why that had happened so many times.

I would be able to continue moving forward on my spiritual journey! I felt greatly relieved to know I could tune into my past without the help of a clairvoyant. Exploring my past lives was an exciting journey that would continue!

Questions:

- I felt like I was making up the scenes I had visualized, but the facilitator said when emotions come in, they provide validation. Does this mean I am beginning to see things like the clairvoyant did?

- I'd always been told I had a good imagination, and was therefore a creative person. Is this why I'm having trouble trusting my *imagination* now?

Spiritual Skills Present: Clairaudience, Claircognizance, Clairempathy, Clairsentience, Clairvoyance, Intuition, Retrocognition

44

Civil War Soldier, 1864

January 10, 1998, 35 yrs.

AFTER A SHORT BREAK, I was ready to continue my spirit work. I still hoped to discover any remaining traumas connected to the issue of body size.

This session would take me into an era which had strangely fascinated me since I studied it in grade school when I was twelve. I'd only been exposed to limited information and seen one movie which took place during the Civil War, so in my mind, the era seemed lovely and romantic. I'd imagined white-columned plantation homes, lush and beautiful gardens, where guests had been welcomed with grace and hospitality. There were lovely ladies who attended balls dressed in flowing gowns, being escorted by admiring gentlemen. The smartly uniformed men were all very gallant and idealistic.

Soldiers were bravely ready to fight to support what they believed in, whether they were wearing blue or grey. I respected General Lee for his ingenuity in sustaining the fight, despite being outnumbered and under-supplied. However, I firmly believed in the principles set forth by the words, "We the People," and the words that followed. If equality and freedom weren't enjoyed by one and all, then these idealistic words lost their power.

I amended my perceptions of the Civil War after taking a history class in college. Learning more of the facts and reading details of the battles quickly replaced my rosy visions with a deadlier, more accurate picture. I realized then that what I had previously thought was an illusion based on fiction rather than truth.

The Civil war started because of several serious issues. But I wondered if the leaders at the time had anticipated the exorbitant costs, in money, lives and pain, which would result because of the war. I assume they must have tried to estimate the possible impacts before marching into battle. But how does one quantify the emotional toll on families, or the outcomes from a country torn apart? How could one possibly estimate the true expenses of trauma, destruction, and death? It was inconceivable. More importantly, how would the deep hurts which continued to exact a price in the present finally be resolved and healed?

I had noticed an apparent pattern relating to warfare in general. It seemed clear that only after both sides had exhausted their supplies, their troops, and their money were the participants willing to sit down and resolve their disagreements. So, why weren't negotiations continued until they found solutions? Was it possible that war could have been avoided? Of course, the outcome of freedom for all had to happen. But the costs and collateral damages from that conflict were much greater than anyone could have anticipated.

That history class had definitely changed my opinion. But my views were even more drastically altered while searching this past life for present-life connections…

***

I'M LYING ON THE GROUND and can't move. I am alive, but lying in a thick carpet of dead bodies. It is dark, so I cannot get a clear view of where I am located on this plain of destruction. The stench is unimaginable, worse than anything I've ever encountered. The heat is oppressive and stifling, unrelieved by the motionless air. Odors of blood, excrement, and rotting flesh mingle with a waft of burned human and natural debris. I am clearly alive and trying to figure out, despite my terror, what is going on around me.

I must have been hit, passed out, and have awakened to this sea of death. I can see campfires not too far off; it is the enemy encamped nearby. I dread they will sense my movements and I will be captured or killed. It is a Union camp, and I have heard horrible things about what happens to their prisoners of war.

I lie here for what seems like days; it is excruciating. It's impossible to get up without being seen because the battlefield of human loss stretches deep and wide. My plan is to try to escape tonight when things quiet down. My body is getting weak from thirst and hunger and the trauma of dealing with what I am surrounded by. I have to get out of here!

My attempt to escape when it gets dark fails. Captured and shackled, I'm shipped off to a prison camp. Some relief comes when I recognize several other soldiers in our group. We are being sent to a camp near the coast. I pray that the rumors I've heard aren't true, and that conditions are better at the camp than what I imagine. As the journey wears on, my hope is slim, and I fear the worst.

Conditions are more dreadful than I had imagined. They confine us, too many of us, in a ramshackle barn. The shelter is minimal, with moldy straw on the floors, no beds, and a few pallets. The worst of it is that there is little to no food. We are all starving to death. My stomach feels like it is eating itself, and though I'm still alive, my body is consuming its own tissues to survive, a painful process for which there is only one relief. The men here are like living skeletons, and I feel very much like I did lying on that battlefield. I'm alive, yet surrounded by death. We move around very little, the stench of unbathed bodies, sewage, and worse, hang in the air. Words cannot describe this living death.

I am lucky to find a friend of mine imprisoned here. It is unfortunate for us to be reunited in this place under these circumstances, but it is so good to talk with him and have his comforting presence. Our friendship is one of the things helping us both to survive.

My friend is quite weak, and I pray he can hold out, but he has been suffering in these conditions for too long. Death may soon take him, but at least then, he will be out of pain. I stay with him. We try to keep our spirits up, but it is no use. Suddenly serious, he tells me to use his body, to eat whatever flesh remains, so I can survive and be free once again. I am horrified beyond words.

My cell mates and I have eaten things we never dreamed of eating as food while in this place; rats, grubs, bugs, disgusting things. We don't speak of it and will never describe the details of our experiences here to our families should we be blessed enough to see them again. To be so hungry feels like a kind of insanity to me.

My friend dies a few days later in my arms. Those of us left honor him as best we can, and then the others prepare his remains. We eat his body; we survive. A few of us live to be released and go home. At last, the physical ordeal is over. But the emotional repercussions are so severe, especially the guilt

I feel about consuming my friend, that they continue on for the rest of my life. I know I did what he wanted me to do, but I will never forget him, nor forgive myself for being so weak, a slave to my stomach.

My friend was right, though. Because of the sustenance of his body, I am able to go on, to live long enough to see the end of the war and return home. But I, like everyone else involved in the war, especially the residents of that camp, will never be the same.

CONCLUSIONS:

This life had been challenging to look at. It was another lifetime where I was forced to compromise my principles and had to eat a loved one in order to survive an appalling situation. It seemed that part of the weight issue I was currently dealing with connected to this life. Starving myself to lose weight in my present had never been pleasant, and with this remembrance clearly etched into my being, I understood why my dislike of hunger pangs had been so intense and intolerable.

Being put in a position of having to eat the flesh of a friend or loved one is a horror few can imagine. When I had first heard the story of the Donner party[1], I felt disgusted and swore that if I were ever in a similar situation, I would die rather than eat my comrades. The convictions I held, my moral fortitude, and my faith in the strength of my spirit were now in ashes. Humbled and ashamed, I knew now that I was not strong enough, not good enough, to stay true to my principles. I knew I had not had the strength to resist the demands of starvation. My survival instincts had been too strong.

In my present life, I had felt very uncomfortable seeing people who were so thin they looked anorexic. An extremely emaciated woman had walked past me in a mall when I was a teenager. She had been so thin that there were no muscles or organs between her jutting hip bones, nor were there any muscles on her bare arms. She had been a walking skeleton without curves or softness, just skin and bones. It bothered me a lot, and now I understood why.

After reliving the vivid realities of this life, war held a far less patriotic appeal to me. The devastating actions and horrific aftermath of the war had created deep wounds, which had affected thousands of people. The conflict had impacted every mind, body, and spirit of those involved in the war. Many changes came about after the war's conclusion. There were new freedoms and opportunities for some. But for others, the changes had given rise to intense hatred and resentments. Wars created deep, invisible wounds in the survivors who carried the emotional traumas forward.

After recalling this experience, I mentally understood how war seemed inevitable at times. But because costs or outcomes could not be accurately predicted, it seemed to me to be a lousy way to resolve conflicts. There would always be a price higher than anyone could imagine at the outset, and therefore, war seemed something to avoid at all costs.

Now more than ever, cooperation and communication, rather than war, seemed a much easier, cheaper, and humane way to resolve the differences between people and nations.

Spiritual Skills Present: Clairalience, Clairaudience,
Claircognizance, Clairempathy, Clairsentience, Clairvoyance,
Retrocognition

[1] — The Donner Party was a group of American pioneers
who, after being snowbound en route to California, reportedly
resorted to cannibalism in order to survive.

45

Master Wood Carver

June 10, 1998, 35 yrs.

MY PRIOR SESSION HAD been upsetting, so I was glad to delay my next excursion into the past. I had more time and energy to devote to my spirit work when school was on summer break. I was grateful my resilience was high when I made time for this next session. This regression was unusual because I experienced physical and emotional symptoms even before I arrived for my appointment.

During my preparations at home, I had been unable to meditate, and unable to sit still. I had always been a calm, quiet person, but on the day of my appointment, I experienced severe anxiety. There was no reason for me to feel restless and nervous. Was my agitation connected to my upcoming session? Was I about to revisit an exceptionally traumatic lifetime? I'd had difficult sessions before, and I'd been in situations of extreme duress, yet I hadn't felt this jittery. My trepidation grew as the time for my session grew nearer. I prayed I would be able to handle whatever I was about to uncover...

***

I ARRIVE EARLY FOR MY SESSION and try to relax. As my appointment time gets closer, I am still fidgeting and cannot sit down while

I wait. I'm pacing the floor until my session starts. This is very unlike me.

We begin with an introductory meditation, yet I am still feeling apprehensive and can't relax. I start shivering as I if I am cold, though I am not physically cold. Even after the facilitator puts a blanket on me, my shivering continues to intensify. What is wrong with me? If this is about what we're going to look at, it must be *really bad!*

As we proceed into my next past life, my shivering does not abate. After some difficulty, I begin to see myself in a small town. The streets are made of stone, dirt, and wood. I am a short, wiry man, wearing a leather vest or apron that has handy places to put tools. I am a shop owner, a master craftsman. I build and carve wood, and sometimes make products out of leather, metal, and other materials. As I continue going further into this lifetime, my teeth start chattering and my shaking gets even worse.

My beloved wife and I live in a small place just outside of town. Every day I walk the path into town to work in my shop. Today, the local pastor comes to the shop and asks me to come over to the church. He wants to talk about the details of a new cabinet they want me to build. As we step inside the door of the church, I know something is wrong. It is unnaturally quiet. Several people are there tending to church business, and when they see me, they turn away.

I look toward to the front of the church by the altar. Something is there. As the priest and I walk forward, my agitation grows. A cloth is covering what seems to be... a body? Without a word of warning, the cloth is removed and to my horror; it is my wife, or what is left of her body.

The pastor quietly says that she was burned in an accident while making candles. Suddenly, a vision of the accident pops into my mind. I can see her tending the fire underneath the large black kettle that we set up to cook down the tallow in the yard. She has her long brown work dress on, a heavy leather apron and her white bonnet tied under her chin. I see her stirring the waxy substance with a large wooden paddle, when part of a log from the fire pops and rolls out toward the hem of her dress. Unbeknownst to her, her dress catches fire. When she notices she panics and inadvertently dislodges one of the kettle supports. It tips over onto her. Trapped, she is engulfed in flames and hot wax, a horrible, agonizing death. Seeing her body now in the church, I am appalled.

Within me, overpowering waves of emotion rush up: raging fury, despair, and profound heart-breaking sadness. I am frozen in irate anguish. Why didn't they warn me, tell me something was amiss, before presenting me with the dead body of my wife? Outwardly, I have lost all expression, apparently taking the news without a word or fuss. Going from being called here for something ordinary to experiencing the destruction of my world is an unbelievable shock. Being told in such a way seems utterly cruel. Why didn't they warn me, tell me something—anything that would have prepared me?

I feel my heart breaking into pieces inside my chest and seem to see it happening at the same time. It seems like I have broken into two people, one who can function and do what is expected, and the other, my emotional self, is withdrawing from the outer world. I see my head nodding; I hear myself saying what is needed, and then watch as I turn and walk from the church stiffly, as if I'm encased in lead. I am numb. My emotions are shutting down. This is more than I can bear. My heart is broken. All the loving dreams my wife and I shared, the future we dreamed of, the children and grandchildren we planned to have and enjoy. All of it is withering away, all gone.

My wife and I had been so lucky, and we knew it. We had shared a love that our friends did not seem to comprehend. They often complained about their spouses, their lives, and their children. Not us. What my wife and I had was irreplaceable, and now she's gone. Without her, my life is empty and pointless.

Everyone is at her funeral. My wife was well loved. She was one of the people who made life heaven on earth, an angel. I feel as wooden as the carvings in my shop. She's gone. She is gone and all I can think to do is that which is familiar, my wood carving. I go back to work. Work is my life now. The rest of what used to be my life is over.

Moving forward in that lifetime, I see my life as the same scene, playing over and over. I am stuck in a rut, mindlessly repeating the routines of each day. Every morning I get up from the cot I sleep in, straighten out the gray wool blanket. I eat the same thing every day and go to work. My wood shop is now my only purpose. It is my comfort and my diversion. The smell of the wood is familiar and comfortable. I create and carve, and then every day I go home and go to sleep, only to do it all again the next day. Each day is like the day before, and tomorrow will be the same as yesterday. I tread the same path for years, my footsteps making the groove deeper and smoother with each day that passes. There is no possibility of changing my course now. I do not know how, nor would I care to try.

Going into my death experience, I see myself going to sleep one night, an old man, and not waking up. But oddly, the next morning I wake up, same as always, and start my day. I get up, feeling a little lighter, but don't think anything about it. It is good to feel better, so I don't question it. I look forward to getting a lot of work done today. I have my breakfast and go to work, the same as usual. My day goes well. I come home and go to bed.

This continues on for some time until eventually the townsfolk question my absence. They seem to think I have not been showing up at my shop. They come to my home and discover my body lying on the cot. But I don't understand why everyone is so upset. I'm still here; they seem to ignore me. I am just fine—same as always. Shrugging it off, I go to work. I do my job and come back home again.

The next morning, I wake up, and I'm not alone. I see a beautiful, glowing lady. She is sitting next to me on my cot. I sit up quickly. She tells me it is time to go, to leave this place and the sorrows it holds. She says that there will be no more pain.

I am confused and don't know what she is talking about. I need to get to work. She tells me that my body has died and that it is time for me to go. I glance back and see my shrouded body lying on the cot, though I am standing right next to her. With growing uncertainty, I argue with her, tell her how ridiculous this all is. Clearly I am still here, still alive, and I have business to attend to, so I leave to go to work, walking the well-worn path I have walked all my life.

I get to work and notice that I can't grab my tools anymore. There are people in my shop cleaning it out. I try to stop them shouting, "It's not right! You can't take my tools! This is my work!" They have no right to take my work, to take away my tools.

The pretty lady appears to me again while I'm in the shop. This time, she is not alone. This time, there is another lovely woman with her. The lovely woman looks very much like my wife did before she died. She is beautiful and has kind eyes, just like my wife. I stare at her intently until it finally dawns on me from her manner and expression that she is my wife!

My wife is alive? How is this possible? But it doesn't matter anymore. I am just so incredibly glad to see her! My feelings, long suppressed, rush up and pulse through me again. The accumulated layers of pain melt away, along with the sorrow and anger that's been keeping me stuck here all these years. My loneliness and bitterness are dissolving, cleansed by the love for my wife that I could not express for so long. I feel healed and at peace. With one more look at my shop, the pretty lady, my wife, and I leave this place. My wife and I are happy and together at last.

CONCLUSIONS:

This had been an amazing session. It was quite different, and I learned many things. My body or my subconscious mind had me restless and shaking even before my conscious mind recalled the events of the past. The shivering had gotten worse the closer I had come to the horror of being presented with the charred body of my wife. When I saw her lifeless form before me, my emotions had escalated to an unbearable level. It was then that I felt my heart breaking into pieces. I had seen an energetic image of my heart actually cracking into fragments, and once that happened my overwhelming emotions became more bearable and my shaking subsided.

At the end of the session, we spent some time energetically transforming some of the trauma. During the transformations, the broken and missing energetic fragments of my heart were retrieved, healed, and restored.

It surprised me that this session had been so clear and that I had been able to view this past life in such rich detail. But even more astounding were the waves of intense emotions that I had felt during the recall of these events. The facilitator had told me before that emotions were a way of validating that I had tapped into an actual past life memory. I sincerely believed that to be accurate after this session. The memories of this past life had not been a jumble of incidents appropriated from my present life. I had felt an extremely intense love for my wife and had felt despair beyond imagining when she was gone. These were not feelings I had experienced in my current lifetime.

It became apparent while reviewing these scenes that there were several emotional behavior patterns in my present that likely had their beginnings during this past life. One pattern is reflected in the relationship I have with my tools. I am a bit obsessive about my tools, and rarely, if ever, allow others to use or borrow them. In the past, I had treated my tools as rare and precious objects. Now I know that the fastidious way I have of cleaning my tools, keeping them well-oiled and organized in my present life may not have been a sign of neurosis or irrationality. I had been a Master Craftsman in the past, whose entire focus and emotional well-being had been connected to woodworking and the tools I had used for that work. That I devoted time and attention to my tools in the present seemed quite logical now, especially having had such a high investment of unresolved emotions connected to my tools and my work. It also seemed reasonable that I would not have loaned my tools to anyone except to someone who would treat them with the same care and respect.

It was incredible to discover that I could trace my emotional reactions to certain smells in the present back to a past life. While visiting old historic missions, both as a child on school field trips and then later with my own child, there was one area of every Spanish Mission that had always disturbed me. I hadn't liked it, and I had no explanation for my intense dislike. I had always been leery of the candle-making rooms, the ones where they made the tallow candles. The monstrous cast-iron tallow pots always gave me the creeps. Just the sight of them was bad, but the smell was worse. I could not stand the smell of tallow, even though it had been centuries since they had made candles there. This past life explained part of the why. It was completely understandable now, after opening this lifetime. Presently I love to burn candles, but only ones that smell good, and nothing that even remotely resembles the smell of tallow.

Additionally, I'd always had a very strong emotional reaction to the smell of wood. No other members of my family did a lot of woodworking, yet I had been drawn to that smell most of my life. Whether it was the smell of freshly cut wood, the lumberyard, unfinished furniture, wood curls from a carving, a Christmas tree, a campfire, or the scent of the forest; I've always experienced a soothing pleasure from the smell of wood. I love it!

There were other habits that connected too. During this past life, I had the habit of working a lot. I worked all the time in order to avoid dealing with how I felt about my wife's death. Work was my solution, my focus, my balm. Work was something to keep me busy and thinking about other things besides my grief and loss. This tactic of using work to distract or suppress feelings seemed to connect directly to my present. I tended to use work now, as I had done when I was a woodcarver. While under stress, I worked more and stayed busier so I did not have time to dwell on unpleasant realities. It had been a habitual present-life pattern, which had some of its roots in the past. But seeing my workaholic habit in action in this past-life showed me how detrimental my avoidance behavior could be and motivated me to re-examine and change this pattern in my present. It seemed like it would be much better to deal with the emotions and the life lessons while they were happening whenever possible.

The biggest surprise was being able to see and experience spiritual fragmentation. The possibility of a heart actually fracturing on a spiritual level had been mentioned to me before, but I had never really believed it and didn't quite understand why it would happen until the recall of this lifetime.

Now I saw that it was a real thing, and how it could be beneficial in the short-term. When faced with an overload of emotions, Spirit had provided an emotional pressure relief valve so that I could survive the situation, then deal with it later when I was stronger. It had helped me to manage for that lifetime and now I had been able to go back during my session, heal the emotions, and restore the broken pieces of my heart and soul. That was something I hadn't been able to do during that lifetime.

Fragmenting had clearly been a temporary solution, and as with all actions, there were consequences which had to be corrected and balanced. I was grateful that this process had enabled me to go back and heal my broken heart.

Spiritual Skills Present: Clairalience, Clairaudience, Claircognizance, Clairempathy, Clairsentience, Clairtangency, Clairvoyance, Divine timing, Retrocognition

46

Rock ON!

July 8, 1998, 35 yrs.

WITH A LIGHTER WORK SCHEDULE in the summer, I had been able to spend more time on my spiritual work. The last session had been heartbreaking, but after a month of journaling and meditations, I was ready to start the next round.

My left shoulder had been hurting, so I added it to the list of subjects I wanted to investigate...

***

I GET INTO THIS SESSION very quickly and get a clear picture without struggling. I am a man walking along with others through a desert towards a walled city. We are being taken to the market to be sold as slaves. After arriving, I am put with the others in a holding pen, which is basically a cage. It is so crowded in here that there isn't room to sit down, only to stand or lean in the sweltering heat.

I am sold along with several others to someone who is completely covered in robes and wearing a head wrap. We walk for a long time to get to a rock quarry located outside the city. There is a long trench dug alongside an enormous block of stone, an obelisk, which we are to continue carving. They put me and the others into the trench and chain us there. We tap and hack away at the stone endlessly, in terrible, inhumane conditions. They do not release us for any reason. The heat and sun are unbearable; the work is excruciatingly difficult and tedious.

I've not been long in the trenches when an accident occurs. An enormous boulder of stone breaks loose from the slope above my position and rolls down toward me. Since I am chained in place, I can do nothing to get out of the way. My first reflex is to raise my arm in a vain effort to protect myself. I should have done something else because raising my arm causes it to get pinned directly under the boulder.

Hideously painful, my left arm is being crushed between the obelisk and the fallen rock. The trench walls are angled, which helps keep the boulder from dropping in and crushing the rest of my body, but hinders the efforts to remove it. My arm is firmly wedged, and I am trapped. I can hear shouting as the other slaves are told to push or pry the boulder out of the trench. But the more they try, the more the rock settles into the trench and onto my arm. They continue prying, and my arm, agonizingly, is getting crushed and mangled with each movement. The pain rises intolerably and I pass out. Somehow, I can see the faces of the other slaves who are trying to get the rock off of me. They are honestly trying to help.

They manage to remove the boulder eventually, but I am no longer in my body when they pull it out of the trench. I am either unconscious or dead; I don't know. The overseers have no concerns about my physical status at all. All they care about is the obelisk, and that it is undamaged. My death, the loss of a slave, does not disturb them in the least. But if the fallen rock has cracked or chipped the huge stone obelisk, they will have to abandon the project and start over, which will cost them dearly in money, time and slaves.

***

CONCLUSIONS:

At the end of that life, I had passed out, gone into shock, and the emotional and physical traumas had fragmented my spirit. This had also happened in the woodcarver's life. Evidently, it was a way of coping with unendurable stress. At this session, the facilitator told me fragmenting often occurs during times of extreme duress and the small piece of soul that splits off contains some of the negative emotional energies associated with the event. He said that the fragment was being cleared, cleansed, and would soon be returned to me. As they restored the fragment, it amazed me that I'd been able to observe the process. The fragment had a beautiful green energy pattern, a piece of me which was good to have back. Facing the trauma of my past had allowed the fragment to be restored.

This life had a cord of energy, which connected to another experience I'd had in the red rock country when I visited there with my friends in 1989. The cord attached to my chest/solar plexus, the same spot in my body where I had experienced those odd pain sensations when my friends and I had first approached one of the energy vortexes. I guess all the rocks and boulders I had seen in that area had triggered a deep memory which caused the odd pains. The pains lessened after I popped into that first past life in the chapel and had completely disappeared when I'd faced the lessons of this lifetime. I had been healed, and I felt more complete and at peace.

Spiritual Skills Present: Astral Projection/Out of Body, Claircognizance, Clairsentience, Clairvoyance, Intuition, Retrocognition

47

Vengeance!

July 15, 1998, 35 yrs.

AFTER THE LAST SESSION, I felt so much better that I wanted to maintain my healing momentum. So I quickly scheduled this session for the following week. I learned that the facilitator had found an intuitive assistant to help with the regression work. There would be a new clairvoyant helping clients to tune into their past lives. I looked forward to working with the new assistant and wondered what she would pick up on...

***

IN THE OPENING SCENE, I see myself as a young South American native woman in the forest gathering nuts, seeds, roots and berries. Absorbed in my work, I do not notice a man wearing a leopard-skin headdress approaching. He attacks me and throws me to the ground. I am fighting wildly, screaming as loud as I can, trying to prevent him from assaulting me further. He pulls a knife, then slits my throat and wrists. Next, he slices down the front of me from the neck down, then rapes me as my blood seeps into the forest floor and my life slips away.

When I pass into my spirit body, I am still furious and remain nearby seeking revenge. I am not sure how, but I am able to put some of my energy into his spear and remain in that object until a battle occurs. When he throws his spear at an enemy, my energy changes the direction and flight of the spear, turning it back towards him. Like a boomerang, it returns and pierces him in the throat. The same place he cut me. Mission accomplished, I exit the spear and wait for his spirit to come into the non-physical dimension where I am. When his spirit emerges, I attack, grabbing energy from his throat and ripping down his front to the groin energetically, just as he had done to me physically. I am definitely *furiously angry*, even in the present, during the session.

CONCLUSIONS:

The deep part of the session ended quickly, but I still felt extreme anger. This had been a strange experience for me. I had not known that a spirit could willingly stay in the physical realm and inhabit a physical object.

After returning to my present life, near the end of the session, the facilitator asked me to give back the energy I had stolen. I felt a great reluctance to do so. As we continued processing the situation, healing progressed, and the anger gradually subsided. As I continued to release the energy and the emotions, it became easier to return the energy fragments I had taken from my attacker. Rarely had I felt so enraged.

They discovered an energy cord in my throat which linked this experience to a person whom I had seen earlier in a previous past-life exploration. It related to the life when I had been a Spanish soldier who had slipped off the side of a cliff. The cord connected to the man who had told me to let go of the cliff (CK). He was evidently the same person who had attacked me in the forest. Perhaps when he had said to let go in that other lifetime, he had also been subconsciously referring to the energy I had taken from him during this South American incarnation. Perhaps this life experience also explained some of his animosity toward me when he was the Spanish soldier.

The energetic objects, the cords and fragments, which had started showing up in the last few sessions, were unusual. I had not seen or heard of these things before. Learning about the existence of energetic cords helped me to understand why I had sometimes felt inexplicable, intense bursts of feelings and recognized people I didn't know. The cords were actual strands of energy which spanned across time and space and connected me to lesson opportunities which I had not yet resolved. They guided me to the people I needed to see and to the places I needed to be. My journey was getting more interesting with each session.

Spiritual Skills Present: Astral Projection/Out of Body, Claircognizance, Clairempathy, Clairsentience, Clairvoyance, Energy Healing, Retrocognition

48

The Camp

January 3, 1999, 36 yrs.

HAVING REVIEWED SEVERAL past lives by this time, I had begun to realize it was unnecessary to recall entire lifetimes, only certain critical scenes. It wouldn't have made sense to explore every detail of every lifetime — that would take an eternity! It made more sense to revisit scenes in past lives where I had lessons yet to learn, so I could review the details which connected to my present.

As usual, I had brought my list of current life situations that I wanted help with. I told the facilitator and clairvoyant what I wanted to work on before we began, to give us a place to start. It couldn't hurt to ask, though it was becoming apparent that Spirit knew exactly what I needed to see next...

I FIND MYSELF ON A TRAIN, in a boxcar crammed full of people. It is noisy, smelly, and I'm surrounded by frightened men with no room to do anything but attempt to stand upright and try not to get trampled. As we come to a halt, the fear increases. I've heard rumors about these camps, nothing good. After the door slides open, they herd us like cattle down the ramp into a holding area.

Our captors order the other men and I about with disdain. They treat us like vermin. Whenever they ask me to do anything, I resist consistently, even though it does not improve my situation. But I just cannot see myself cooperating with these automatons that treat me as a senseless beast rather than as a human being.

I am worried about my wife. They separated us at the start of all this, when she was forced into a different boxcar. Once I lost sight of her, something in my heart froze. I am afraid for her more than I am for myself. I don't know if I will ever see her again. But I cannot allow myself to dwell on it, and I will not cooperate with the villains that keep us apart. I am going to do anything and everything I can to fight them.

They have taken from me, from all of us, everything of value: watches, rings, jewelry, clothes, and gold fillings. Even the women's hair is being cut off to be used in wigs. We are lucky to be herded into a large tiled room where they hose us down with disinfectant and stale water. Then they give us uniforms to wear so we can toil in their workhouses and factories. The unlucky ones aren't flooded with water, but with gas. They never walk out again.

When I get a chance, I attempt to escape, but do not succeed. This lands me in the worst job imaginable. Actually, no decent person could ever imagine this. But to conceive it, you would have to understand the people who brought us here. My captors are very innovative about letting nothing go to waste. They use us to do their work and are also using us in their experiments for their scientific research. They treat us like rats, or worse than rats. When they are done abusing us, they remove every useable bit from their human cattle, our hair, teeth, and skin, and then throw what is left of us away.

My job is to remove the skin from other dead humans by operating a machine my captors developed for that purpose. They make human leather from the skins and use it to make things. These are my former friends and neighbors, my spiritual brothers and sisters. I do not willingly do this disfiguring work. I am beaten often, quite enthusiastically. Being here, I am forced to learn to block my emotions and suppress my conscience in order to do such things to others, even though they are already dead. Every moral fiber of my being revolts at the very idea of what I am being made to do, but I manage by not looking at the faces and by trying not to think about what I am doing. There is only one thought that inspires me to survive: my hope that my loving wife and I might be reunited and escape this nightmare.

If we can get out of here someday and regain our lives, maybe we can try to forget some of this hideousness. It is a very slim hope, but I can manage a lot with hope and thoughts of my wife. My hope is like the light from a match in a darkened room, small but effective. I survive by living moment to moment. I never allow my thoughts to stray to the future or to dwell in the past.

This works until the day the unthinkable happens. As my eyes scan the new body placed before me at my station, I recognize the familiar, well-loved body of my wife. I freeze. I can't move. Horror strikes me, not only because my once beautiful wife is now before me—dead, but that I am being told to deface her body in the worst possible way. I can't. I won't.

They whip me, and I still do not move. I will not move. Never again. This is the last straw. I don't care what they do to me now. My tiny spark of hope is gone, like the light in my wife's eyes. Eventually, they realize that no amount of beating will get me to move or cooperate. The only response I give—just once—is to yell in my language, "This is my wife, you bloody bastards!" I never speak another word.

My strength, which has served me well all my life, now becomes a liability in that place. They decide to use me for tortuous experimentation. How long can a human body tolerate being in freezing water, and how cold is too cold? This is what they want to know. At first I am shivering violently, and then my muscles do not seem to function at all. My body survives what feels like a long time. My mind grows numb and I am unable to recognize how much time has passed. I remember chunks of ice floating by my face in the dark, freezing water. Soon I cannot stay afloat. Nauseous and numb with cold, I finally die.

***

CONCLUSIONS:

After coming out of that lifetime, the outrage I had suppressed during my last hours rose up in me after my death, similar to what I had felt in a previous session. I stole spiritual energy from one of the soldiers who had killed me and was frankly surprised I had not done more in retaliation.

How could people have done such heinous things to other humans and forced others to do terrible things as well? It was incomprehensible to me. I still could not fathom what kind of twisted thinking had made it seem okay to inflict such insane cruelty on others. To force people to do such unspeakable things to each other, physically, mentally and emotionally, was in every way an abomination against God and the beauty of His creation. It took a lot of effort to calm down, release all the emotional trauma of this lifetime, and allow healing to occur.

I had done some releasing of the traumas that came up during my session. But it would take much longer to process and come to terms with these memories. Over the next few years, I'd found that I needed to go back into these scenes from my past. By reviewing these events during meditation and allowing the old thoughts and feelings to come up, I was able to discover residual buried traumas, yet unresolved. If anything was still upsetting to me, expressing my sentiments and journaling about them brought them into the light and allowed me to view the situation differently. Allowing myself to receive insights and loving support from my guides, and asking Spirit to uplift my heavy emotions, were also essential parts of the releasing process. This technique proved very effective in helping me to accept traumatic situations and forgive those who had hurt me. But I still had much to learn about how to view things from a higher, broader perspective.

While examining my experiences, questions kept popping into my mind. What if I had chosen the roles I had played in each of my various lifetimes? What if everyone else had also chosen? Maybe some souls had played vicious roles so that other souls could learn how to deal with challenging circumstances and people. Dealing with nice people was not very difficult. What if everything that had happened was, from God's perspective, perfect, balanced, and just?

My questions remained unanswered, but eventually I hoped everything would become clear. For now, I felt like I needed to learn to accept and love all the people and situations I had experienced in these lifetimes. Once I accepted that my lives had unfolded exactly as needed, and affirmed that all would become clear in time, I became calmer, and knew I had learned some of my lessons. I felt healed. It had been quite difficult for me to accept these events in a loving way at first.

Reviewing the events and going over the lessons of this lifetime had been an essential part of the releasing process for my anger, sadness and all the other stuck emotions. The man I had been in that lifetime had reined in his feelings so tightly that multiple layers of emotional armor had to be peeled away. It took quite a lot of time and effort, but I felt much better after clearing all that emotional debris.

After this life review, I'd heard rumors in the media denying that the holocaust ever happened. How could anyone say that the stories from survivors and witnesses were only propaganda? Or that millions of deaths hadn't occurred? Their implications that the horrors of my experiences hadn't really happened struck me deeply. My fury rose up, fresh and intense in response to these horrific lies. I had to remind myself that I had chosen all my experiences as opportunities to learn from, even the hearing of rumors. However, my reaction had made it clear that I needed to continue working on releasing and healing these deep emotional wounds.

In this past life, I had also learned that even in situations where it seemed I had no choice, I could still choose how I responded. No matter what they took away from me, or what they inflicted upon me, I had still made choices. I suppose I could have obeyed orders and complied with every humiliating thing they had asked me to do so that I might have physically survived. Maybe it had been my pride, my conviction, my beliefs, or a combination thereof that had kept me from giving in to my captors' demands. But when it came right down to it, I could not sacrifice every shred of respect for myself. Without self-respect, a physical existence would have been like being alive, but dead inside.

Another part of the lesson had to be about the amazing, motivating power of love. Because when all my other concerns and emotions had been stripped away, the strongest motivational force, for me, had been love. I had been able to manage anything asked of me until the death of my wife. My reason for living, my flickering flame of hope, had been snuffed out once she had died, murdered. I had no reason to try anymore, because I had lost my love.

I came out of this recall with stronger convictions about standing up for what is right. After the suffering I'd experienced and the atrocities I had tolerated, I felt that part of the lesson of that life had been to more quickly recognize the importance of taking action against anything that violated respect and freedom.

I'd also learned to question and fight anything that subjugated or harmed any segment of humankind. My past circumstances had been created because the world had tolerated the actions of an inhumane leader and his supporters. Rather than stopping them, it seemed as though people had waited for someone else to take action, not realizing that that kind of passive inaction was the same as support. Standing up and defending my rights, and saying what I needed to say, still challenged me in my current life. It took nerve to challenge the status quo.

I could also see that some of my experiences connected to my present, particularly my intolerance for the cold. I had never enjoyed swimming in cold water and definitely did not find it invigorating, though some people had tried to convince me that it was good for my health. Jumping into cold water was something I detested. The shock and discomfort of it was not nearly worth whatever health benefits I might receive. After this session, my attitudes did not seem as irrationally random as they once had.

Having to unearth and release unhealthy thoughts and feelings which had been suppressed for so long had been difficult. It had become clear to me that bottling up my emotions had not been an effective way of dealing with them. Granted, in this particular situation, suppression had been a necessary tool for survival. But if I had survived the camp, how many years would it have taken me to release the traumas if had I been able to release them at all? Maybe my lessons had worked out for the best after all.

Spiritual Skills Present: Clairaudience, Claircognizance, Clairempathy, Clairsentience, Clairvoyance, Divine timing, Retrocognition

49

I am he...

January 30, 1999, 36 yrs.

As HAD BECOME MY HABIT, I'd started a guided meditation prior to going in for my regression. It helped me to relax, clear my mind, and focus on what I needed to explore next. The meditation had me go to my sacred space, which I returned to whenever I wanted to receive loving support and wise guidance from Spirit.

My place included a beautiful meeting room where my invited guests and I could comfortably sit and chat. Spirit guides and others entered through a special doorway, which allowed only positive beings to come in. Meeting my spiritual advisors in this sacred space had made it much easier to communicate with them. Sometimes it felt as if the messages I received from Spirit were coming from me. But my doubts would fade after reviewing the numerous details and inspirational content. It seemed unlikely that the information had come from my mind. Still, it would allay any of my residual doubts and fears if I could be certain of who I was talking to.

It had been suggested that I could verify that my visitors were of the light by surrounding them with a bubble of pure white God energy. In the realms of Spirit, anything surrounded in light became light. When I added that process to my meditation practice, I felt safer and more certain I was communicating with high-level beings.

That afternoon, I asked my guide Achaeus for help with my current dilemmas. Some of my issues continued to puzzle me. Classical music playing in my head prompted me to ask about my long-time preoccupation with Tchaikovsky's music. It had been seventeen years since the tune from that music box had so haunted me, yet my fascination had remained strong. Every piece of music by that composer seemed familiar, though I had no conscious recollection of having heard them before. When I had a lot of stress happening in my life, his music, coincidentally, always seemed to come on the radio at just the right time. Listening to his music usually helped me to calm down and often brought a sense of reassurance.

After he had advised me about my other inquiries, my guide had a clear and simple response to my question about Tchaikovsky. He said,

"What if you ARE Tchaikovsky?"

My denial and disbelief quickly rushed up in response to his answer. There was no way I could have been him! That had not been the answer I had expected or wanted. How many stereotypes had I heard about New Age people bragging to others about how they had been a famous person like Cleopatra or Joan of Arc in a past life? To me, that was a play for attention similar to the people who said they knew somebody famous in order to feel self-important. That was not how I wanted to boost my self-esteem. I was not into sensationalism, nor was I looking for attention.

But... if what my guide had said was true, it might explain the odd incidents related to the music I'd heard over the years...

No. I still couldn't believe it! Definitely not. My intentions for doing past life work had always been for spiritual growth and healing. It had never been my goal to boost my ego by claiming to have had a famous past.

I had met celebrities in my present life, had seen others at the airport or in restaurants, and to me, they were just people, like me. The only difference was that many people had heard of them. I had concluded years ago that if I were to become famous, I would want people to respect my privacy, so I had always respected the privacy of the celebrities I'd been around.

The discussion of the composer dropped, and my guide and I talked about other things. Hopefully, my meditation had sufficiently prepared me for my session. I wanted to maximize the time available for recalling the past...

***

AFTER I ARRIVE, we get quickly into the session. I see myself as the prisoner in that horrible camp again. Often, I am brought back to a lifetime I have already visited so that I can finish clearing any residual energies and emotions that still need resolution. After we complete the healing on that life, we begin the next.

I see myself, a young boy who is having trouble sleeping. I hear music loudly playing over and over again in my head. The music is keeping me awake. I am upset and cry out repeatedly,

"Make it stop, make it stop!"

My mother tries to comfort me, but I cannot calm down with the constant sound assaulting my senses. I don't understand what is happening and don't know how to stop it.

In the next scene, I am the same boy, now grown into an older adult, sitting at a piano, playing softly. I am sad and frustrated. After working on a musical phrase for a while, I stop playing, fold my arms and rest them on the piano. My head soon drops onto my arms, resigned. I can see it so clearly and the feelings of despair are so intense, it's almost too much to bear.

The clairvoyant stops me and asks if I recognize who I am. I realize, with such a vivid recollection and uprush of feelings, that I am Pyotr Ilyich Tchaikovsky (PT), as my guide had tried to tell me. Seeing these images and sensing PT's feelings make this intensely real to me and hard to deny. As I feel his emotions and sense his thoughts, I am shocked to the core. If my guide had not introduced this idea to me ahead of time, I would have been completely overcome. Oh, my dear God... this cannot be happening!

As the session continues and I start to accept the potential reality of this discovery, I begin to feel a sense of relief. To finally understand why all his music seems familiar is incredibly helpful. I'm not crazy! All the confusing feelings of déjà vu, the times I had sung along to songs I didn't know, the haunting sadness of the music box, now suddenly is clear and makes perfect sense.

As I allow myself to step fully into that life, I know I love my mama very deeply, even though she doesn't always understand what is really going on with me. I am her sensitive boy. She knows I am unhappy and often distraught, but she does not fully comprehend what is happening to me any more than I do. Playing music on the piano soothes me more than anything else.

Expressing myself with that instrument also allows me to feel a sense of emotional relief with each note, since music can express emotions that cannot be described with words. While I am playing, I go into a meditative state where the clamor of my thoughts can finally quiet down. The music playing constantly in my head temporarily fades into the background, and I experience moments of peace.

As Tchaikovsky (PT), I feel like I never have the words to express what I am sensing and feeling. I'm almost constantly overpowered by all that I feel and see, the music, the spirits, and the voices I hear. Even if I could describe what I sense, my family and community would never understand or accept it. Besides, if I were to say more about what I see and hear, I might be locked up permanently with the other people who are dangerously insane.

Eventually my mother, not knowing how else to help me, bows to social pressure and sends me away to school. Little does she know the truth of what really goes on within those hallowed halls. It is not the happy place they say it is. While I am at school, I quickly learn to keep quiet on certain subjects so that I can keep my freedom.

The only time I feel truly free is when I am playing music. All my other daily concerns, worries and anxieties fall away and I am flung into a world of peace, where I am lovingly visited by beautiful Angelic Beings. I tell no one about my experiences with these music Angels, and I never describe them to the adults at the school. So precious are the Angel spirits to me. I fear that if I mention them, the Angels might not return and I will lose their calming support. It is my association with these Beings that helps me to write music. Some songs come from the music the Beings bring to me and sometimes I expand on their ideas. Other pieces come from the music in my head, which never ceases. It is always, always, always playing.

***

CONCLUSIONS:

Though my guide had told me about PT prior to my session, and though I had experienced part of his life during my appointment, I still found it difficult to accept the idea that I was this person, Tchaikovsky. My brief glimpse into his lifetime prompted me to begin a search of all the books, magazines, and any other information I could find in bookstores and libraries. I wanted to find some kind of proof that what I had seen in my session was accurate. I wanted to verify some of the details and I wanted to know what had actually happened in PT's life, since I knew nothing about it. But so far, it seemed impossible to find unbiased information. I had found that many authors were rather judgmental in their descriptions, their prejudice clearly apparent in the material they wrote. Many writers condemned Tchaikovsky for his apparently odd mental behavior and his sexual preferences.

I had assumed that one advantage of having a famous lifetime was that there would be lots of specific, factual information which could help me validate what I had experienced. I'd hoped to discover intimate details about his daily life and habits. The biographical information I'd found appeared in anthologies about famous composers. These volumes contained brief highlights about his education and a timeline of the major events of his life. A list of his more well-known compositions usually followed. My search through such books wasted my time and elicited nothing useful. I needed to know about what he thought, what he struggled with, who he was as a person. These kinds of personal details I had been unable to find.

The resources I'd unearthed, I had found irritating and hurtful. It would've been so much better if authors could have written their accounts without adding their personal biases. A skilled writer should be able to convey factual information without depicting their subject in a scornful light. How could a writer judge someone they had never met?

The events in PT's life were often distorted or blown out of proportion. Some articles portrayed him as an oddity, sensationalizing the simplest things in order to sell more papers. One account reported that, while conducting a concert, PT held his head because he was afraid it would roll off his shoulders. With such accounts, it did not surprise me that their version of Tchaikovsky depicted a sad, strange human being.

Of course, none of the resources I'd found mentioned, or even hinted that PT may have had heightened intuitive abilities. PT had talked about Angel Beings that helped him with music. But even PT had said he told no one about them, so it made sense that I found nothing. I also needed to consider that in his time, there would be fewer sources of information. To get the details I wanted, I would need first-hand accounts from people who knew him, or maybe personal papers PT himself had written. Public access to private information like that seemed unlikely. Even if those sources had been available, PT would likely never write down his private thoughts out of fear of discovery.

Since I hadn't found reliable, unbiased information or any first-hand accounts, it seemed like it might take a while to verify the details I'd picked up during the PT session, if I ever could. My inability to confirm what I had sensed sent me into a deep depression, halting my progress and stopping me from exploring further. *I did not want to be Tchaikovsky!* However, I could have accepted it more easily if I'd been able to prove it to myself.

But if I could not verify the accuracy of what I'd seen, how could I continue with my regression work? Had I taken a wrong turn? Had I been imagining all these traumatic past-life events? Was I making up my connection to the Tchaikovsky lifetime? Why was my inability to find acceptable proof connected to this lifetime causing me to so severely doubt myself and re-think all my prior experiences? Part of me knew I had to keep going. I had to complete the journey. Now, more than ever, I really needed answers. But after this regression session, I felt powerless, as if I had hit an enormous, immovable wall.

Opening the PT lifetime had struck a deep chord within me. I had felt so connected to his music for so long. I hoped there would be some way to understand why I had been shown this lifetime. How did it connect to my current life? There were a couple of things that PT had mentioned which seemed similar to me in the present. One was how he felt while playing the piano. I'm sure my piano skills weren't even close to his, but, like him, I felt at peace while playing. Being able to play an instrument, especially the piano, brought me clarity, allowed my mind to rest, and soothed my soul. I could also totally relate to the constant playing of music in his mind. That was my plight as well. There was a constant stream of music and lyrics running through my head all the time! But I could dismiss as coincidence hearing music in my mind and feeling relaxed while playing the piano, because many people also experienced such things. These were similarities, not proof. There had to be some definite way to know if I really had been Tchaikovsky.

This past life was different. I would never choose to make up such a fantastical tale as being someone so famous, yet this famous lifetime had emerged. Why had this come to my attention? I hadn't doubted the validity of all the other lifetimes. Why could I not accept this one? Why was I so shaken up by this past life? I had seen so much, so many traumatic events. Yet sensing the lifetime of a boy with music stuck in his head was the one that disturbed me the most? Maybe I had picked up on PT's doubts about his sanity, and it was amplifying my own doubts and fears. Maybe I reacted so strongly because PT had experienced traumas in his life, and tuning into these memories was like opening a can of worms?

Unquestionably, there had to be more to PT's story. Perhaps as more details came to light, I would understand why I felt triggered by these memories. I would definitely need to do more sessions in order to get clarity about this lifetime. In the meantime, I was still reeling over the discovery of these past life memories. Never had I imagined that an average person like me could have been such a famous figure. How would I ever come to terms with it? I told no one I had been Tchaikovsky. My moods alternated between excitement about the connection, to depression that I didn't have his talent, to terror that someone might find out and think me delusional or ridiculous. I felt like I was in over my head.

I don't know why I was having trouble accepting that I had been PT. I guess I was afraid of being judged. If I told others I had had a famous lifetime, I assumed they would consider me one of those new-age weirdos. I would never be taken seriously, and my work, my story, would be disregarded as the fantastical imaginings of a lunatic. That's why I wanted proof—why I needed proof. If I couldn't prove to myself, at the very least, that I had really been Tchaikovsky, then maybe I was delusional. Opening this lifetime had triggered a spiritual existential crisis. I was overwhelmed. Somehow, I needed to prove to myself that my spiritual experiences were real.

The confusion lasted a long time. I had continued to search for evidence that would prove I'd actually been this insanely famous person. If I could validate even one unique piece of information, something I could not have known any other way, that would be helpful. But my doubts were so severe that it would be years before I did regression work of any kind. My stubborn curiosity would certainly not allow me to give up for good. I was still resolutely determined to find the answers I sought. I just needed to step back for a bit, let these ideas rest so time and thoughts about other things would help me clear my head. Somehow, someday, my journey would continue...

Questions:

- This life exploration raised many questions: Who and what kind of person was Tchaikovsky?

- Had any of the events I saw in this session actually happened, and could I find a way to verify them?

- Where could I possibly find intimate details like these and be assured of their accuracy?

Spiritual Skills Present: Clairaudience, Claircognizance, Clairempathy, Clairsentience, Clairvoyance, Retrocognition

50

Epilogue, Volume 1

MY SEARCH FOR ANSWERS to the mysteries in my present had brought up so many unexpected past lives! I could never have predicted that my life journey would lead me down this path. I'd started out so fearful and shy as a child. Being sick with asthma and allergies had added to my sense of being different, and my body seemed to echo the emotional strain. But those same illnesses had brought me to desperation and had driven me to ask for help from a God I wasn't sure existed. I never dreamed that my direct question would elicit such an amazing, life-altering response. I hadn't anticipated that. Actually, I'm not sure what I'd hoped for, but I certainly hadn't expected a miracle!

My insatiable curiosity, sparked by those miraculous events, had driven me to persevere relentlessly in search of answers. The amazing thing was. I had been finding them! In facing my pain, bringing it out into the light, patterns seemed to be emerging. It was as if knowing what first caused my pain and fear somehow lessened the severity of it, and I'd been able to heal those deep wounds more readily.

I had discovered that the déjà vu experiences, the nightmares, and the irrational fears, which had impacted me in my present life, had clear connections to traumatic events in my past lives.

Things, places and people had seemed familiar to me because they were well known to me in other lifetimes. My fears and nightmares, which had originated from prior life traumas, no longer had the power to hurt me. Now that I knew their source, my fears had faded, and the nightmares had never returned.

My explorations into the past, both on purpose and by accident, had changed my perspective and values. The difficulties of life seemed less random and rather more like lessons, opportunities for me to master the truth of who I really am. I now knew that I was here to learn about universal concepts, and about the relationships between myself and my family, friends and acquaintances. Facing my past, bringing my prior lives up to a conscious level had been painful and risky, but the risk had been worth the gain. I had received so much!

I had discovered some unique insights about who I was and how I came to be that way. Some of my inexplicable attitudes and feelings made sense now. I had gained a greater understanding of myself and my emotions. By releasing my fears, I was free to reveal my true self more than I had ever done before in my present life. The relief I felt after reviewing the past and coming to terms with the painful traumas and buried emotions was apparent. Many of my fears were gone. Remembering, reliving and releasing my experiences had brought me a greater sense of peace and contentment.

The moments of pure joy and love I had felt in the past were difficult to describe, yet the memory and the feelings had carried through to bless my current life. I knew now that I was capable of having deeply loving relationships, and the possibility that such loving connections really existed gave me great hope.

It was harder to judge others harshly, since I had, myself, been both "good" and "bad." I had belonged to many different races and cultures and had been devoted to several religions. I had experienced the pros and cons of every gender and sexual orientation. I'd lived in the bodies of males and females, had died old and died young. I had committed suicide, been murdered, I had drowned, I'd been starved, burned, abused, beaten, raped, and tortured, and had done much of the same to others. I'd also known great joy, friendship, connection and love, love so deep that it survived, even after bodily death.

My remembrances had brought me profound healing and greater awareness. My fears about death and dying, which had previously terrified me, no longer existed. I no longer felt lonely or alone. Insights had come from all the lifetimes I had revisited. Whether the life was unremarkable, discouraging, tragic, or uplifting, each life brought awareness and gratitude. I felt enriched by my memories.

The opening of that last life, the life of Tchaikovsky, had brought answers to what had been for me a 17-year-old mystery. I knew at last why PT's music had seemed so familiar—because some part of me had written it. I had received a few answers and a little relief from opening up that life. But a whole slew of additional questions had also arisen, along with some sincere doubts about my purpose in doing this work. I needed time to re-examine my intentions to make sure they were in alignment with my values. Once I sorted that out, I would be ready to go on to what came next.

It would be three years before I felt ready to continue, but I would move forward on my journey. I would persist in improving my present by salvaging insights from my past. For decades to come, I would persevere in discovering the answers

I needed. I would continue to gain clarity from the events of my past, and I would keep peeling away the layers to help myself find relief in the present. I wanted more proof, and I was going to get it.

The journey continues...

Moving forward from here...

EVERY EVENT I'VE INCLUDED in this book series has a purpose, though the reason may not be readily apparent. In reading my books...

- I hope to inspire you to discover the purpose of the *coincidental* intuitive events *you* have experienced in your life.

- I hope to encourage you to expand your direct connection to your soul self and Spirit. The key is being consistent. Development practices like meditation and creative expression are fun ways to relax and connect. As your connections become clearer, the information coming from your Higher Self and Source can provide you with amazing assurance. We are all supported by loving beings of light such as Spirit Guides, Angels & Ascended Master Teachers. No middle-man is needed. These and other wonderfully supportive Beings of Light are a reliable source of guidance whenever you need it.

- I hope to show that life events are not random or accidental, but are the result of pre-life planning, free will, and the natural outcome of your own thoughts, beliefs, and feelings. Such events provide you with needed lessons directed by the Divine. They are blessings in disguise.

- I hope to assist you on your journey to free yourself from any self-imposed limits, so you know you can create the life you wish. When you ask, you receive (help, answers, support and comfort). The energy of thoughts and feelings create your world, your reality.

- I hope to inspire you to follow your dreams, pursue self-knowledge, take an active part in your growth, and seek your *own* answers...

- I hope to assure you that you are *worthy* of all the joy and happiness you seek.

- I hope to provide evidence that we are all connected at a spiritual level, an indivisible part of Source.

I welcome your comment and questions. I would enjoy hearing how my story has helped you.

With Love, Adria

AdriaGaebriallaAuthor@gmail.com

AuthorAdriaGaebrialla.com

Appendix A – Questions Answered!

This is a quick-reference guide to show which chapters hold the answers to some of my questions. Many mysteries were solved! Other insights were discovered later in my journey, beyond the time span covered in this first volume (see subsequent volumes). Of course, there are answers which I am still seeking...

Section One – Fear and Uncertainty

Section Two – Disbelief to Possibility

Section Three – Tentative Proof

<u>Chapter</u>   <u>— Connects to Chapter</u>

Appendix B – Intuitive Skills Listing

Quick-reference guide

At the end of each chapter, there is a list of Spiritual skills that were present during the described events.

For your convenience, the skills are listed here, along with the chapter numbers where you can read additional examples of each skill.

Intuitive Skill — Chapters where experienced/explored

Astral Projection/Out of Body — 7, 29, 46, 47

Auras — 5, 9, 30

Automatic writing — 31

Clairalience — 7, 21, 29, 34, 44, 45

Clairaudience — 6, 7, 13, 21–31, 33, 34, 36-45, 48, 49

Claircognizance — 2, 3, 5-8, 13-17, 19-21, 23-25, 27, 28, 31-35, 37-40, 42-49

Glossary

THESE ARE MY SIMPLIFIED *definitions for the convenience of the reader. Please check your dictionary and other resources for additional information.*

Astral Projection (Out of Body) – Thought to be the 'Astral' body leaving the physical dimension, exiting the physical body and traveling to other places and dimensions in the universe. The Astral body remains connected energetically to the physical body.

Aura reading – The ability to intuitively perceive the energies and colors surrounding the physical body (using clairvoyance), and to describe what the energies indicate.

Automatic writing – An intuitive ability that allows the higher self or another spiritual being to convey it's thoughts by physically writing a message using the intuitives' physical body. I feel there are two levels to this. The first level is a type of *channeling* where the host is in a level of trance and writing down what they are sensing clairaudiently; retaining control of their physical body and consciousness. The second level is a type of *mediumship* where the host allows another spiritual being or entity to control their physical body in order to receive thoughts and messages directly from the consciousness of the visiting being.

Chakra – Centers of energy in various locations throughout the human body. It is generally agreed upon that these energy centers are located in alignment from the top of the head to the base of the spine. The primary centers are identified as the: root, sacral, solar plexus, heart, throat, third eye, and crown chakras. (*Some say a chakra can be located anywhere a channel of energy intersects with another channel of energy in the subtle body; therefore, chakras may number from 144 to 88,000*).

Channeling – The ability of a person to sense and relay information from spiritual or other dimensional beings using the intuitive senses, while remaining consciously in control of their own physical body. (*see also Medium/Mediumship*)

Clairalience (*'clear smelling'*) – The ability to perceive distinctive odors (smoke, perfume, foods) which do not have a source in the present physical dimension; smelling something which is beyond what can normally be perceived with the olfactory senses.

Clairaudience (*'clear hearing'*) – The ability to perceive sounds, music, or voices, which do not have a source in the present physical dimension; hearing something which is beyond what is normally sensed by the human auditory system.

Claircognizance (*'clear knowing'*) – The ability to become aware of knowledge and events without using any other tangible means or resource (technology, prior experience).

Clairempathy (*'clear feeling'*) – The ability to become aware of the emotions of other people or objects. To be able to feel others' emotions and distinguish them from the one's own feelings.

Clairgustance (*'clear tasting'*) – The ability to perceive distinct tastes or foods (sweet, bitter, sour, cigars, metal, Grandma's Rum Cake) which do not have a source in the present physical dimension; tasting something which is beyond what may normally be tasted by the human sensory organs.

Clairsentience (*'clear awareness'*) – The ability to tune into energies and other non-physical dimensions which are normally undetectable by human senses (i.e. energetic connections, cords, vibration/frequency, future and past-life connections (déjà vu), awareness of other physical and non-physical beings through intuitive sensing). Also recognizing synchronicity.

Clairtangency (*clear touching'*) – The ability of a person to perceive information about others on a physical level (pain, hot, cold, itchy) which does not have a source in the present physical dimension of the intuitive; these sensation(s) do not originate with, nor do they belong to the intuitives' physical body.

Clairvoyance (*'clear seeing'*) – The ability to perceive visually, representations (pictures, colors) of beings, objects, situations or energies which do not have a source in the present physical dimension; visualization; seeing that which is beyond what can normally be perceived by human eyes/sensory organs; intuitive sight using the *third or pineal eye.* (experienced like recalling memories of a place you've been)

Divine timing – The belief that everything is happening or unfolding at the most perfect moment possible, and in accordance to a higher plan of Spirit/God.

Energy Healing – One of several modalities which can detect the energies in the body(s) and facilitate the release of energetic blockages, resulting in an improved state of health and well-being in the physical, mental, emotional and/or spirit body(s). (Reiki, Acupuncture, Chinese Medicine, Reflexology, Massage, Yoga, etc.)

Intuition – The ability to sense beyond what is thought to be the normal five senses of sight, sound, touch, smell and taste; extrasensory perception; use of the various 'Clair' senses (see above).

Medium/Mediumship – A person who allows the consciousness or energy of another spirit or being to use and control their physical body so that the spirit may convey information directly; the host is often not consciously aware of what the visiting spirit is saying or doing. (*see also Channeling*)

Precognition – The ability to predict through extrasensory means (not aided by experience or any other resource) events which have not yet occurred.

Psychometry – The ability to receive information from objects through intuitive means; receiving intuitive information by physically touching objects; related to Clairtangency.

Retrocognition (*backward knowing*) – The ability to intuitively gain information and/or experience situations and events which occurred during a current or prior life incarnation; gaining knowledge about events in the past, which could not have been ascertained or inferred by any other normal means (unconnected to present life memories or experience).

Subtle bodies – The seven energetic layers (or bodies) said to emanate from the physical body in correspondence to the seven primary Chakras including: etheric, emotional, mental, astral, etheric template, celestial, etheric. [*Alternatively, it is* *thought that there are four lower bodies (physical, emotional, mental and etheric or memory) and three higher bodies (intuitive, spirit, causal)].*

Synchronicity – When events occur which seem to be connected or orchestrated, yet no clear causative structure is apparent; meaningful coincidences.

Telepathy – A type of clairaudience; the ability to intuitively hear and comprehend the thoughts or ideas of others.

Recommendations...

Books

ALEXANDER, THEA. 2150 A.D. New York: Warner Books, 1976.

Prophet, Mark L. & Elizabeth Clare Prophet. *Saint Germain on Alchemy: Formulas for Self-Transformation*. Gardiner, MT: Summit University Press, 1985, 1993.

Orin (Spirit), Sanaya Roman & Duane Packer (Mediums). *Spiritual Growth: Being Your Higher Self (Earth Life Series: Book 3)*. Novato, CA: H J Kramer, 1989.

Roman, Sanaya & Duane Packer. *Creating Money: Attracting Abundance (Earth Life Series: Book 5)*. Novato, CA: H J Kramer, 1988, 2008.

Weiss, Brian. *Many Lives, Many Masters: The True Story of a Prominent Psychiatrist, His Young Patient, & the Past-Life Therapy That Changed Both Their Lives*. New York: Fireside, 1988.

https://www.regressionassociation.com/spirituality/reincarnation/books

Spiritual Regression Therapists

Spiritual Regression Therapy Association.
https://www.regressionassociation.com/

About the Author

ADRIA HAS BEEN LEARNING and applying spiritual teachings to help herself heal and develop since 1978. After 40+ years of exploring and clearing her own past, she now assists others in finding answers.

Adria is a Spiritual Regression Therapist, Intuitive Reiki Master, and Spiritual Channel/Medium. She also has certifications in Between Lives Regression, Advanced Energy Management, and Hypnotherapy. She has a bachelor's degree in kinesiology and a Master's in Education.

Adria hopes that by sharing her journey, she will help inspire growth and healing. Her Spiritual Retreat Center also provides an uplifting, supportive environment where people have the freedom to relax, heal, and explore.

Find out more about Adria at AuthorAdriaGaebrialla.com.

From Disbelief to Assurance, Vol. 2

The Journey Continues...

Sign up for my mailing list to be informed of new releases and special offers:

http://AuthorAdriaGaebrialla.com

or

http://BrightHeartPublishers.com/

The adventure continues as I discover more lifetimes and dive deeper into a few we've already taken a peek at!

More spiritual explorations, more mysteries solved... more amazing proof.